The Harried Housewife's Cookbook
(Easy, Quick and Delicious Recipes for the Busy Household!)

The Harried Housewife's Cookbook
(Easy, Quick and Delicious Recipes for the Busy Household!)

by Cynthia O'Connor O'Hara

Upstate Publishing
New York

The Harried Housewife's Cookbook
(Easy, Quick and Delicious Recipes for the Busy Household!)

By Cynthia O'Connor O'Hara

Published by Upstate Publishing, Post Office Box 16, Whitesboro, NY 13492-0016 U.S.A.

Manufactured in the United States of America

Illustrated by Stephanie Farina

Library of Congress Catalogue Card Number 96-90605

ISBN 0-9654385-0-3

Dedication

To my mother, Janice O'Connor, for teaching me from the time I was a child how to create "something" from "nothing," and for giving me the best gift a parent can give a child.... independence.

To my father, Myles O'Connor, for instilling in me a strong belief in family, and for always being there.

To my husband, Michael O'Hara, for his unconditional love, support and devotion, and for being the best father in the world.

And especially to my daughters, Colleen and Kelly, my two Greatest Blessings. This book could not have been written without you.

CONTENTS

Acknowledgments

Special thanks is extended to Stephanie Farina, Illustrator of *The Harried Housewife's Cookbook.* Stephanie worked tirelessly trying to "capture" the real Harried Housewife and her two children, Colleen and Kelly. She actually came over and sketched on a typical, harried day. The front cover is representative of an average day. Thanks again, Stephanie. You did a great job.

Many thanks goes to the staff at the Dunham Public Library, Whitesboro, New York, for all their guidance and help in locating necessary books. Also, a warm thank you to my dear friend, Kathy Rabbia for always listening and just being there.

A tremendous amount of thanks goes to my family and friends for all they have contributed to help bring *The Harried Housewife's Cookbook* into fruition. I sincerely appreciate it.

Introduction

This book is written and designed for every harried person. Whether you are a man or a woman, work in the home or out of the home, are a novice or a pro at cooking, this book is written with you in mind.

It is geared toward the busy, on-the-go person who would like to prepare homemade food more often but doesn't have the time it takes for extensive meal preparation. The recipes are made from ingredients found in a typical kitchen, thus eliminating the need for any speciality shopping. For this reason, it will also appeal to those watching their budget.

This is an easy-to-follow cookbook with delicious recipes that can be made in a short amount of time, allowing you to spend more time with your family and friends. The recipes are clear and concise, with the detailed information needed to get you from start to finish. They are written so <u>anyone</u> can follow them.

The recipes will generally serve four to six, unless otherwise specified. If, for example, a particular recipe calls for chicken breasts, it may simply state, "2 chicken breasts, skinless and boneless." It does not state the exact amount of weight for each breast due to the fact that, for these particular recipes, it does not matter the exact weight. It is designed for ultimate ease in the kitchen, thereby allowing you to quickly prepare a meal with little or no forethought, using what you already have in the kitchen.

This unique cookbook takes a whimsical approach to practical cooking. It takes a lighthearted look at everyday life as exemplified by frequent sayings from The Harried Housewife. The annotations under each recipe are sometimes serious and sometimes silly but always true. One thing is for sure, cooking for your family and friends will never be the same again!

This cookbook is intended for you to use frequently. As you prepare these recipes for family and friends, keep in mind that the best part of any meal is sitting down at the table, talking and enjoying each other. And remember, as my mother always told my two sisters, my brother and myself as we were growing up, "Take good care of each other. You're all you've got." She's right.

Enjoy!

Cindy
(a.k.a.) The Harried Housewife

The Harried Housewife's Cookbook
(Easy, Quick and Delicious Recipes for the Busy Household!)

APPETIZERS

APPETIZERS

ARTICHOKE DIP
(This is an especially tasty dip that is creamy and warm from the oven. Be sure you have plenty of cold drinks as nothing tastes better with this!)

1 small onion, chopped
1 (14 oz.) can artichokes
(not marinated), drained
and chopped
1 1/2 c. Mozzarella cheese,
shredded

1/2 c. mayonnaise
1/2 c. Parmesan cheese
1/2 tsp. salt

Preheat oven to 350°. In a large bowl, mix together all ingredients. Put into a 1 1/2 quart baking dish. Cover and bake 30 - 35 minutes. Cool in dish 3 - 4 minutes before serving with assorted crackers.

BARBECUED CHICKEN WINGS
(These tasty wings are easy enough to make for a party. Make ahead and keep warm in the oven until guests arrive. They're also great with pizza!)

24 chicken wings
1 c. honey
1 c. soy sauce

1/4 c. lemon juice
4 Tbsp. Worcestershire sauce
1 clove garlic, minced

Preheat oven to 325°. Place chicken wings in a 9" x 13" baking dish. In a large bowl, mix together all ingredients. Pour over wings. Cover and bake 1 hour. Serve immediately.

APPETIZERS

CURRIED CHICKEN TEA SANDWICHES
(These little appetizers have just enough spice for a unique flavor.)

1 (5 oz.) can chunk chicken
in water, drained
1/4 c. mayonnaise
1/4 c. green (Spanish)
olives, minced

1/2 tsp. curry powder
paper-thin olive slices (for
garnish)
loaf of whole-wheat cocktail
(party) bread

In a large bowl, mix together all ingredients except paper-thin olive slices. Spread about 1 teaspoonful of mixture on one piece of bread. Top with olive slice.

DEVILED HAM TEA SANDWICHES
(These easy-to-make hors d'oeuvres are delicious. Place them on a decorative platter alongside Curried Chicken Tea Sandwiches and Shrimp Tea Sandwiches for casual or formal entertaining.)

1 (4 1/2 oz.) can deviled
ham
1/2 c. cream cheese,
softened
1/4 c. dill pickles, finely
chopped

1 Tbsp. onions, finely chopped
loaf of white cocktail (party)
bread

In a large bowl, mix together all ingredients. Spread about 1 teaspoonful of mixture on one piece of bread. Garnish with a little parsley, if desired.

DRIED BEEF DIP WITH RYE BREAD
(This dip is delicious as is, but for a different flavor, leave out the dried beef and add one tablespoon dill weed. Tastes great with rye!)

1 (16 oz.) container sour
  cream
1 1/2 c. mayonnaise
6 oz. dried beef, finely
  chopped

2 Tbsp. parsley
2 Tbsp. dried, minced onions
loaf of rye bread, hollowed out

In a large bowl, mix together all ingredients. Refrigerate until ready to serve. Put dip into bread and serve with chunks of rye.

DRIED BEEF AND OLIVE SPREAD
(The Spanish olives add a zesty flavor to this delicious appetizer.)

1 (8 oz.) pkg. cream cheese,
  softened
2 Tbsp. mayonnaise
1 (3 oz.) pkg. dried beef,
  finely chopped

1/4 c. green (Spanish) olives,
  chopped
1 tsp. dried, minced onions

In a medium bowl, mix together cream cheese and mayonnaise. Stir in chopped beef, olives and onions. Refrigerate until ready to serve. Serve with assorted crackers.

APPETIZERS

FRIED WALNUTS

(The great thing about these delicious walnuts is that they can be made two weeks in advance and stay fresh in a closed container. This is especially appreciated during the holiday season when time seems to get away from us, and people are always stopping by!)

6 c. water
4 c. walnuts
1/2 c. sugar

1/4 c. sesame seeds
1/4 c. vegetable oil
salt as desired

In a large pan, boil water. Add walnuts and cook 1 minute. Rinse walnuts with hot water and drain. Add sugar to warm nuts and stir until sugar is dissolved. (If necessary, let stand 5 minutes to dissolve sugar.) In a large frying pan, heat oil over medium heat. Fry nuts in batches for about 5 minutes. In a separate, small frying pan over low heat, cook sesame seeds until they are heated thoroughly, stirring often (a nonstick frying pan works best). Place well-drained nuts in heated sesame seeds and toss gently. Sprinkle with salt as desired.

ONION DIP

(This is your basic, homemade dip that goes great with chips, pretzels or crackers. It tastes so good, it won't last long!)

1 (16 oz.) container sour
  cream
1 1/2 c. mayonnaise
2 Tbsp. dried, minced
  onions

2 Tbsp. parsley
1/2 tsp. salt

In a large bowl, mix together all ingredients. Refrigerate until ready to serve.

Tip: You may substitute plain yogurt for sour cream, if desired, without sacrificing the flavor.

SHRIMP DIP WITH CRACKERS
(This is an all-time favorite! Whenever I host a party, this is the most-requested appetizer of all. It is so easy to make, they will think you went out of your way!)

1 large can shrimp
1 (8 oz.) pkg. cream
  cheese, softened

cocktail sauce*
crackers

In a medium bowl, mix together shrimp and cream cheese using a fork. Form into a ball (freshly washed hands work best!). Cover and refrigerate. When ready to serve, place shrimp and cream cheese ball on a serving platter. Pour cocktail sauce over. Serve with assorted crackers.

*COCKTAIL SAUCE

3/4 c. ketchup
1 Tbsp. horseradish

1 tsp. lemon juice
1/2 tsp. salt

In a medium bowl, mix together all ingredients.

SHRIMP TEA SANDWICHES
(These are delicious little hors d'oeuvres! Again, they will think you spent all day in the kitchen. Only you will know the truth!)

1/4 pound medium-size
  shrimp, peeled and
  deveined
1 small celery stalk,
  finely chopped

1/2 c. mayonnaise
4 drops hot pepper sauce
loaf of white cocktail (party)
  bread

In a medium pan, boil water and add shrimp. Cook 1 minute or until shrimp turn opaque. Finely chop shrimp. In a small bowl, mix together shrimp and celery. Blend in mayonnaise and hot pepper sauce. Spread about 1 teaspoonful of mixture on one piece of bread. Garnish with a little parsley, if desired.

ZUCCHINI SQUARES

(These delicious squares can go anywhere. They can be a scrumptious appetizer or served with dinner for a tantalizing treat!)

3 c. zucchini, thinly
 sliced
1 c. Bisquick
1/2 c. vegetable oil
1/2 c. onions, finely
 chopped

1/2 c. Parmesan cheese
4 eggs
1 clove garlic, minced
2 tsp. parsley
1/2 tsp. oregano
1/2 tsp. salt

Preheat oven to 350°. Lightly grease a 9" x 13" baking pan. In a large bowl, mix together all ingredients. Spread in prepared pan. Cover and bake 25 - 30 minutes. Cool 5 - 7 minutes before cutting into squares.

THE HARRIED HOUSEWIFE SAYS....
The key to a happy home is a happy mother.

SOUPS, STEWS, SALADS

SOUPS, STEWS, SALADS

AMBROSIA
(This fresh salad is delightful alone or for a delicious change, serve atop pound cake.)

2 large oranges, peeled
1 1/2 c. fresh peaches,
  sliced
3/4 c. red seedless grapes,
  halved

1 c. coconut
3 Tbsp. sugar
1 c. orange juice
1 banana, sliced

Cut the oranges into 6 slices each then quarter. In a large bowl, toss together all the fruit except the banana. Add the sugar and orange juice and toss again. Cover and refrigerate until ready to serve. Just before serving, add the banana.

CHICKEN SALAD
(This is a good way to use leftover chicken. The Italian salad dressing keeps this salad from being dry while adding extra flavor. You may add 1/4 cup chopped celery, if desired.)

4 c. cooked chicken,
  chopped
2 tsp. onions, finely
  chopped

3/4 c. mayonnaise
2 Tbsp. Italian salad dressing
1/2 tsp. salt
1/4 tsp. pepper

In a medium bowl, toss together chicken and onions. In a separate, small bowl, mix together the mayonnaise and salad dressing. Add salt and pepper. Add to the chicken mixture, stirring gently to coat chicken well. Serve on lettuce leaf or as a sandwich.

CORN CHOWDER

(This is an old family favorite. Whenever I make this, I fondly remember making it for my brother and two sisters. It seems like only yesterday that we were all sitting at the dining room table enjoying this old-fashioned chowder on cold, winter days. It sure leaves you with a warm feeling.)

1 pound bacon, chopped	1 can cream-style corn
1 medium onion, chopped	3 c. milk
4 medium potatoes, peeled and diced	3 Tbsp. butter
	salt to taste
1 can corn, drained	pepper to taste

In a large pan, over medium-low heat, cook the bacon slowly until the pieces are brown. Pour off all but 2 tablespoons of fat. Add the onions and cook 5 minutes. Add the potatoes and 3 cups water. Cover and cook until the potatoes are tender. Add both cans of corn and milk and cook 5 minutes more. Before serving, add the butter, salt and pepper to taste. Enjoy!

CREAMY BROCCOLI SOUP

(Pair this up with homemade Cornbread and you will have any easy, delicious meal.)

1 c. ham, chopped	3 Tbsp. flour
1 c. water	1 c. Swiss cheese, cubed
1 (10 oz.) pkg. frozen, chopped broccoli	1/2 tsp. salt
	1/4 tsp. pepper
2 c. milk	

In a medium pan, boil ham in water 10 minutes. Add broccoli and cook until tender. In a small bowl, gradually add milk to flour, stirring until well blended. Slowly add milk mixture to ham mixture, stirring constantly until mixture slightly thickens. Simmer 5 minutes, stirring occasionally. Add cheese, salt and pepper. Cook until cheese begins to melt. Serve immediately.

CREAMY FRUIT SALAD
(This fruit salad is so good, even children love it!)

1 medium-sized can
crushed pineapple,
not drained
1 medium-sized can
fruit cocktail, drained

1 c. miniature marshmallows
1 (3.4 oz.) pkg. instant pistachio
pudding
1 pt. whipping cream

In a medium bowl, mix together crushed pineapple, fruit cocktail and marshmallows. In a separate, large mixing bowl, beat together whipping cream and pudding until thickened and peaks form. Add contents of first bowl and mix well. Cover and refrigerate until serving.

CROCK POT STEW
(This is just what you need to come home to after a long day! The best part is, you can put everything into the crock pot in the morning and it will be ready just in time for dinner!)

2 - 3 pounds stew beef
4 medium potatoes, peeled
and quartered
4 medium carrots, peeled
and quartered
1 medium onion, peeled
and quartered

tomato juice (to almost cover)
instant tapioca (2 Tbsp. per
pound of meat)
1/2 tsp. salt
1/4 tsp. pepper

Combine all ingredients in a crock pot. Turn pot on medium and cover. Cook 6 - 8 hours.

EGG AND OLIVE SALAD
(The olives add a much needed flavor to an otherwise boring egg salad!)

3/4 c. mayonnaise
2 tsp. mustard
1/2 tsp. salt
1/4 tsp. pepper
1/2 c. green (Spanish)
 olives, chopped

1/3 c. green peppers, finely
 chopped (optional)
8 hard-boiled eggs, diced

In a medium bowl, mix together mayonnaise, mustard, salt and pepper. Add olives, green peppers and eggs. Gently toss to mix. Serve on lettuce leaf or as a sandwich.

FRENCH ONION SOUP
(This is such a flavorful soup that having one bowl is not nearly enough!)

3 Tbsp. butter
4 c. onions, thinly
 sliced
5 tsp. beef boullion (or
 5 cubes)
salt to taste

pepper to taste
4 slices toasted French bread
4 thin slices Provolone cheese

In a large pan, over medium heat, melt butter. Add onions and cook until transparent. Add 4 cups of water and boullion. Simmer, partially covered, 30 minutes. Add salt and pepper to taste. To serve, spoon soup into ovenproof bowls and float a piece of bread with cheese on top. Bake in a 350° oven until cheese is melted, about 5 minutes. Serve immediately.

GERMAN POTATO SALAD

(This is an old recipe that has been in our family for years. The authentic flavor cannot be matched by any other German Potato Salad recipe I have tried. You will need to saute' the onions in the bacon fat to obtain the best flavor. Just remember, you don't do it that often so why not live a little! This is so good, it's worth it every now and then! Also, keep in mind to serve this particular salad warm, after letting it stand a couple of minutes, to truly derive the taste of the Old Country!)

6 medium potatoes	1 1/2 tsp. salt
8 slices bacon	1/2 tsp. celery seed
1/2 c. onions, finely	1/4 tsp. pepper
chopped	1/2 c. cider vinegar
2 Tbsp. flour	1/2 c. water
1 1/2 tsp. sugar	

Boil potatoes in jackets. Peel and slice thin. In a large pan, over medium-low heat, slowly fry bacon. Drain on paper. (Crumble when cool.) Reserve 2 tablespoons bacon fat and saute' onions in fat until golden brown. Blend in flour, sugar, salt, celery seed and pepper. Stir in vinegar and water. Bring to a boil, stirring constantly. Boil 1 minute, stirring constantly. Carefully stir in potatoes and crumbled bits of bacon. Remove from heat and cover. Let stand until ready to serve. Enjoy!

THE HARRIED HOUSEWIFE SAYS....
It really doesn't matter what you feed your family, just that you all sit down together at the table as often as you can.

HAMBURGER SPINACH SOUP
(You probably already have all the necessary ingredients in your kitchen to make this delicious soup!)

1 1/2 pounds lean
  ground beef
1 medium onion,
  chopped
2 cloves garlic,
  minced
1 (28 oz.) can tomatoes,
  chopped

1 (10 oz.) pkg. frozen chopped
  spinach, thawed
6 c. water
6 tsp. beef boullion (or 6 cubes)
1/4 tsp. pepper
1/2 c. rice, cooked

In a large pan, over medium heat, brown beef with onions and garlic, stirring often. Drain, if necessary. Add tomatoes with their juice, spinach, water, boullion and pepper to beef mixture. Bring to a boil. Reduce heat, cover and simmer 20 minutes, stirring occasionally. Add rice, cover and simmer 10 minutes more. Serve immediately.

IRISH STEW
(There is nothing better than the smell of homemade stew wafting through the air. They will think you spent all day on it!)

2 Tbsp. shortening
2 pounds boneless shoulder
  of lamb, trimmed and
  chopped into 2" cubes
2 c. boiling water
2 medium carrots, chopped

1 c. white turnip, cubed
2 medium potatoes, peeled and
  cubed
1 medium onion, chopped
1/2 tsp. salt
1/4 tsp. pepper

In a large, heavy pan, over medium heat, melt shortening and add lamb. Brown well on all sides. Stand back and pour 2 cups boiling water over lamb as it will sizzle and sputter. Cover and simmer 1 hour. Add all other ingredients. Cover and simmer 30 minutes more. Serve immediately.

ITALIAN MACARONI SALAD
(This salad is full-of-flavor. You can have it any time of year, but seems to go especially well during the hot, summer months, particularly with a backyard barbecue or picnic.)

1 pound spiral macaroni, cooked, drained and cooled
1 c. Provolone cheese, cubed
1/2 c. pepperoni, sliced
1/2 c. black olives, sliced
1 vine-ripened tomato, chopped

1/4 c. Parmesan cheese
3 Tbsp. olive oil
3 Tbsp. wine vinegar
2 Tbsp. fresh basil, chopped (or 1 tsp. dry basil)
1/2 tsp. salt
1/4 tsp. pepper

In a large bowl, toss cooled pasta with remaining ingredients. Cover and refrigerate until ready to serve.

KIELBASA STEW
(An easy enough stew that has that delicious, homemade taste!)

1 pound polish kielbasa, coarsely chopped
1 (28 oz.) can tomatoes, chopped
4 medium carrots, peeled and chopped
4 medium potatoes, peeled and chopped

1 large onion, chopped
1 (9 oz.) pkg. frozen corn
4 c. water
4 tsp. beef boullion (or 4 cubes)
1/2 tsp. salt
1/4 tsp. pepper

In a large pan, add kielbasa and cover with water. Bring to a boil. Reduce heat and cook until tender. Drain and return to pan. Add tomatoes and their juice and all other ingredients. Bring to a boil. Reduce heat, cover and simmer about 20 minutes or until vegetables are tender. Serve immediately.

LEMON-LIME JELLO SALAD
(Another favorite! Both children and adults alike will enjoy this not-too-sweet salad, especially when they find the bananas and marshmallows hidden inside! This salad travels well and would be great to bring for a pot-luck dinner.)

2 (3 oz.) pkgs. lime jello
2 c. boiling water
1 (8 oz.) can crushed
  pineapple, drained
1 (3.4 oz.) pkg. instant
  lemon pudding

1 c. milk
1/2 pt. whipping cream
1/2 tsp. sugar
4 firm bananas
1 1/2 c. miniature
  marshmallows

In a large bowl, dissolve jello in boiling water. Stir in crushed pineapple. Pour into a 9" x 13" pan and chill until set, about 2 hours. In a medium bowl, mix together pudding and milk. In a separate, large mixing bowl, beat together whipping cream and sugar until peaks form. Fold pudding into whipped cream. Cover and refrigerate until jello is done setting. When set, slice the bananas and place on jello. Cover with marshmallows. Spread pudding mixture over marshmallows. Chill several hours before serving.

THE HARRIED HOUSEWIFE SAYS....
You can eat off my floors! There's always a variety to choose from! Anything from dehydrated vegetables and a choice of cereals to reconstituted milk and dried meats! Have a ball!

MACARONI AND TUNA SALAD

(My mother's recipe! We always had tuna in our macaroni salad. I never had it any other way until my later years and still prefer it this way. You can also make three hard-boiled eggs, chop two and add to the salad, slice one and place on top. Garnish with a little paprika, if desired.)

1/2 pound elbow macaroni, cooked, drained and cooled
1 (6 oz.) can tuna, drained and flaked
1/2 c. black olives, sliced (optional)

1/4 c. onions, finely chopped
1 c. mayonnaise
2 Tbsp. milk
1/2 tsp. salt
1/4 tsp. pepper

In a large bowl, combine macaroni, tuna, olives and onions. Gently toss to mix. In a separate, small bowl, mix together mayonnaise, milk, salt and pepper. Add to the macaroni mixture and gently stir to mix well. Cover and refrigerate until serving.

THE HARRIED HOUSEWIFE SAYS....

If you see me with my lips pursed,

you will know I'm dying of thirst!

And you can bet, I'll surely plead,

a bottle of wine I really need!

MUSHROOM STEW

(This thick, hearty stew tastes great with fresh Italian bread or warm garlic bread. If you prefer, you may buy fresh mushrooms already sliced. However, I would not recommend using canned mushrooms!)

1 1/2 - 2 pounds loose Italian sausage, hot, medium or mild
1 large green pepper, chopped
1 large onion, chopped
2 cloves garlic, minced
1 (28 oz.) can tomatoes, chopped
1 (28 oz.) can crushed tomatoes

2 (8 oz.) pkgs. fresh mushrooms, stems removed and coarsely chopped
2 tsp. beef boullion (or 2 cubes)
1 tsp. basil
1 tsp. parsley
1 tsp. oregano
salt to taste
pepper to taste

In a large, heavy pan over medium heat, brown sausage with peppers, onions and garlic. Drain liquid. Add chopped tomatoes and their juice and all other ingredients plus about 1 cup of water (depending on consistency). Bring to a boil. Reduce heat, cover and simmer 1 hour, stirring occasionally. May be served over macaroni or as is, with your choice of bread. (Tastes even better the next day!)

THE HARRIED HOUSEWIFE SAYS....
The best way to get yourself motivated into finally cleaning the house is to invite company over!

ORANGE DELIGHT SALAD
(This salad has a gentle, light flavor of oranges, accented by a creamy layer of lemon. Out of this world!)

2 (3 oz.) pkgs. orange
  jello
2 c. boiling water
2 c. mandarin oranges,
  drained
1 c. crushed pineapple
  with juice

1 (6 oz.) can frozen orange
  juice
1 (3.4 oz.) pkg. instant lemon
  pudding
1 c. milk
1/2 pt. whipping cream
1/2 tsp. sugar

In a large bowl, dissolve jello in boiling water. Stir in oranges, pineapple with juice and orange juice. Pour into a 9" x 13" pan and chill until set, about 2 hours. In a medium bowl, mix together pudding and milk. In a separate, large mixing bowl, beat together whipping cream and sugar until peaks form. Fold pudding into whipped cream. Cover and refrigerate until jello is done setting. When set, spread pudding mixture on jello. Chill several hours before serving.

OYSTER STEW
(This is another delicious and simple old-fashioned recipe. Again, this improves with standing.)

1 qt. milk
3 Tbsp. butter
1 pt. oysters

salt to taste
pepper to taste

In a double boiler, heat milk. In a large pan, over medium heat, melt butter. Add oysters and cook until tender. Add salt and pepper to taste. Stir in heated milk and simmer 15 minutes, stirring occasionally. Do not overheat. Serve immediately.

POTATO SALAD

(This salad tastes a little different than the potato salads most of us have grown accustomed to. The Spanish olives and Italian salad dressing add a zesty flavor to what might have been an otherwise bland salad. This is great to make for a picnic, barbecue or when you have company, but may be easily cut in half to serve just four to six.)

8 medium potatoes,
  peeled and quartered
4 hard-boiled eggs,
  coarsely chopped
1/2 c. green (Spanish)
  olives, chopped
1/4 c. onions, finely
  chopped

1 1/4 c. mayonnaise
3 Tbsp. Italian salad dressing
1/2 tsp. salt
1/4 tsp. pepper
1/4 tsp. paprika

Boil potatoes until just tender when pierced with a fork. Drain. As soon as you can handle them, peel and dice. Place in a large bowl and cool. Add eggs, olives and onions and gently stir. In a separate, medium bowl, mix together mayonnaise, salad dressing, salt and pepper. Gently fold into potato mixture until all pieces are coated. Sprinkle with paprika. Cover and refrigerate until serving.

THE HARRIED HOUSEWIFE SAYS....
You can bet the day you decide you are not going to do your hair or put on make-up is the day your long-lost friend stops by for a visit!

THREE BEAN SALAD

(This is a delicious salad that is a great accompaniment to just about any dish. You may use any other kind of bean in place of any one of these, or even mix together three completely different types. To give it more of an Italian flavor, omit the onions and add two cloves of garlic, minced along with 1/2 tsp. oregano, 1/2 tsp. basil and 1/2 tsp. parsley. If possible, try to use all fresh beans as this makes all the difference in the world!)

1 can green beans,
  drained
1 can yellow wax
  beans, drained
1 can red kidney
  beans, drained

1/2 c. onions, finely chopped
1/2 c. olive oil
1/2 c. wine vinegar
1/2 c. granulated sugar
1 tsp. salt

In a large bowl, mix together three kinds of beans and onions. In a separate, medium bowl, mix together oil, vinegar, sugar and salt. Pour over beans and toss well. Cover and refrigerate several hours before serving.

WALDORF SALAD

(This is a classic recipe that is easy to make and tastes great!)

2 firm, ripe, green
  apples, cored and
  quartered (with
  skin left on)
1 firm, ripe, red
  apple, cored and
  quartered (with
  skin left on)

1 Tbsp. lemon juice
1 c. celery, coarsely chopped
1/2 c. walnuts, coarsely
  chopped
1/2 c. mayonnaise
2 Tbsp. honey
Iceberg lettuce

In a large bowl, combine apples with lemon juice. Toss well. Add celery and walnuts. Cover and refrigerate. In a separate, small bowl, mix together mayonnaise and honey until smooth. Add to the apple mixture and toss. Serve on a bed of lettuce.

ZUCCHINI STEW

(This is another stew guaranteed to call them in from outdoors with the smell of fresh zucchini and mushrooms simmering in a pot with sausage and tomatoes and just enough spice. Nothing says homemade cooking better than this! A good, crusty bread with real butter is a must.)

1 pound loose Italian sausage, hot, medium or mild
1 small onion, chopped
2 cloves garlic, finely chopped
1 (28 oz.) can tomatoes, chopped
1 (28 oz.) can crushed tomatoes
1 medium zucchini, coarsely chopped

1 small pepper, chopped
1 (8 oz.) pkg. fresh mushrooms, sliced
1 tsp. beef boullion (or 1 cube)
1 tsp. basil
1 tsp. oregano
1 tsp. parsley
1/2 tsp. sugar
1/2 tsp. salt
1/4 tsp. pepper

In a large pan, over medium heat, brown sausage with onions and garlic. Drain. Add chopped tomatoes and their juice and all other ingredients plus about 1/2 cup water (depending on consistency). Bring to a boil. Reduce heat, cover and simmer until zucchini is tender, about 25 - 30 minutes. Serve immediately. Tastes even better the next day!

THE HARRIED HOUSEWIFE SAYS....
Don't wait for company to arrive to open that bottle of wine!
Enjoy a little nip before they are due. After all, you deserve it!

VEGETABLES

VEGETABLES

BAKED BROCCOLI
*(This is a good dish for people who are not too fond of broccoli.
The creamy texture will help them forget they never liked it!)*

2 (10 oz.) pkgs. frozen
  broccoli
1 can cream-of-mushroom
  soup
1/4 c. milk
1/4 c. onions, minced

1/2 c. Cheddar cheese, grated
1/2 tsp. salt
1/4 tsp. pepper
4 Tbsp. butter
1 c. seasoned stuffing mix

Preheat oven to 350°. Lightly grease a 1 1/2 quart casserole. Cook broccoli according to package directions. Drain and put into prepared casserole. In a separate, small bowl, mix together soup, milk and onions. Pour over broccoli. Sprinkle cheese on top. Sprinke salt and pepper over cheese. In a small pan, over medium heat, melt butter and stir in stuffing mix. Spread over cheese. Cover and bake 30 minutes. Serve immediately.

BROILED TOMATOES WITH CHEESE
(These are absolutely delicious! They may be serve hot or cold.)

4 large tomatoes
1 Tbsp. butter
1 c. bread crumbs
1/2 c. Parmesan cheese
1 clove garlic, minced

1 tsp. oregano
1 tsp. basil
1/2 tsp. salt
1/4 tsp. pepper

Preheat broiler. Cut the tomatoes in half and arrange them cut side up in a shallow, buttered baking dish. In a small frying pan, over medium heat, melt butter and add bread crumbs, stirring to coat well. Remove from heat. In a medium bowl, add buttered bread crumbs and all other ingredients. Mix well. Sprinkle evenly over tomatoes. Place under broiler, watching carefully, until crumbs brown and tomatoes heat slightly. Be careful not to overcook.

CREAMY MASHED POTATOES

(These are a delicious change from the usual mashed potatoes. A quick and easy dinner might include Creamy Mashed Potatoes, Chicken, Creamy Paprika and a green vegetable. Prepare Chicken according to directions and place it in the oven first. Then prepare Creamy Mashed Potatoes and place alongside Chicken. They both should be done around the same time. By putting at least two different dishes in the oven around the same time, you will not only be utilizing all available oven space, but will also cut down on utility costs as well.)

6 medium potatoes,
  peeled and quartered
4 Tbsp. butter, melted
1 (4 oz.) pkg. cream
  cheese, softened

1/2 c. sour cream
2 Tbsp. onions, finely chopped
1 tsp. salt
1/4 tsp. pepper
1/4 tsp. paprika

Boil potatoes until tender. Drain. Preheat oven to 350°. Butter a 1 1/2 quart casserole. In a large bowl, mix together butter and cream cheese. Add potatoes and mash. Blend in sour cream, onions, salt and pepper. Pour into prepared casserole. Sprinkle with paprika. Cover and bake 45 minutes. Serve immediately.

THE HARRIED HOUSEWIFE SAYS....
If a lengthy conversation with a "negative" person leaves you feeling less than happy too, limit these conversations as much as possible. Day-to-day life can be harrowing enough without "extra" negativity!

GOURMET BAKED ACORN SQUASH
(These add a nice touch to a dinner table. A must-have for the holiday season or to enjoy anytime.)

3 acorn squash, halved
  and seeded
4 Tbsp. butter
1 1/2 c. unpeeled apples,
  diced

2/3 c. celery, diced
1 1/2 c. bread crumbs
1 c. Parmesan cheese
1/2 tsp. salt
1/4 tsp. pepper

Preheat oven to 400°. Place squash halves, cut side down, in a baking pan in a small amount of water. Bake 20 - 30 minutes or until almost tender. In a large frying pan, over medium heat, melt butter. Add apples and celery and cook 5 minutes. Stir in bread crumbs, Parmesan cheese, salt and pepper. Turn squash halves; fill with apple mixture. Bake 10 - 15 minutes more or until squash halves are tender. Serve immediately.

GREENS
(This is by far the best recipe for preparing greens. The authentic Italian flavor is remarkable.)

2 pounds escarole
1/2 c. olive oil
1/2 pound prosciutto
5 hot or sweet cherry
  peppers, coarsely
  chopped

2 cloves garlic, minced
2 c. water
2 tsp. chicken boullion
1 c. seasoned bread crumbs
1/2 c. Parmesan cheese

Boil escarole until limp. Drain. In a large frying pan, over medium heat, add olive oil, prosciutto, peppers and garlic. Cook until tender, about 5 minutes. Remove ingredients from pan leaving olive oil. Add to the olive oil, escarole, water and boullion. Cook over medium heat 5 minutes, stirring occasionally. Add peppers and prosciutto mixture. Cook 5 minutes more. Stir in bread crumbs and Parmesan cheese. Remove from pan to serving dish. Serve hot.

GREEN PEPPERS, CORN AND ONIONS
(This is another easy dish you can make on the spur-of-the-moment. It requires little or no forethought because you probably already have all the ingredients in the kitchen!)

1/4 c. olive oil	1 1/2 c. corn, cooked
1 Tbsp. butter	1/2 tsp. salt
2 large onions, cut into thin slices	1/4 tsp. pepper
2 large green peppers, cut into thin strips	

In a large frying pan, over medium heat, add olive oil and butter. Cook until butter is just melted. Add onions and peppers and cook until tender, about 5 - 7 minutes. Stir in the corn, salt and pepper. Cook 5 minutes more. Serve immediately.

THE HARRIED HOUSEWIFE SAYS....
Isn't it amazing that the day you decide to drag your kids with you to the grocery store is the day the lady ahead of you in line has a fistful of coupons (expired) and has to write a check, to boot!

MASHED SWEET POTATOES

(These have such a delicate, sweet touch that even children love them!)

4 sweet potatoes,   1 tsp. brown sugar
  peeled and quartered   1/2 tsp. cinnamon
2 Tbsp. butter   1/4 tsp. salt

Put potatoes into a pan and cover with cold water. Bring to a boil. Reduce heat and cook gently until tender, about 15 - 20 minutes. Drain. Place potatoes in a large bowl and add all other ingredients. Mash until smooth. Serve immediately.

MASHED TURNIPS

(This is another recipe that has been in our family for many years. We always enjoy it on Thanksgiving Day with plenty of butter and salt and pepper. The most difficult part of preparing this recipe is peeling the turnips, but it is worth the minor inconvenience.)

1 1/2 pounds yellow   2 Tbsp. butter
  turnips, peeled and   1 tsp. salt
  coarsely chopped   1/2 tsp. pepper

Put turnips into a pan and cover with cold water. Bring to a boil and cook briskly until soft. Drain well. Place turnips in a large bowl and add all other ingredients. Mash until smooth. Serve immediately.

POTATO CROQUETTES

(This is a great way to use up leftover mashed potatoes! Once you try these, you will always want to make extra mashed potatoes, just so you can make them again!)

2 c. mashed potatoes	4 Tbsp. flour
2 eggs	1 c. seasoned bread crumbs
1/4 c. onions, minced	1/2 c. olive oil

In a large bowl, mix together potatoes, one egg and onions. Shape the potato mixture into 8 balls. Cover and chill. In a small bowl, add the remaining egg and slightly beat with a fork. Dip the potato balls into the flour, shake off any excess, dip into the egg and then into the bread crumbs. Place potato balls on a plate. In a large frying pan, over medium heat, add olive oil and cook until just heated. Add the potato balls and cook until they brown, several minutes. (Turn the heat down if they brown too quickly.) Turn them frequently to make sure they brown on all sides. When done, place the croquettes in a baking dish and cover. Keep warm in a 300° oven until ready to serve.

POTATO PANCAKES

(This is another old-fashioned recipe that tastes just as good now as it did then! If you enjoy recipes from our grandparent's and great-grandparent's generation, this one is especially for you.)

3 medium potatoes, peeled and freshly grated	1 Tbsp. flour
	1 Tbsp. heavy cream
	1 egg, beaten
2 Tbsp. onions, finely chopped	1/2 tsp. salt
	1/4 tsp. pepper
1 Tbsp. green peppers, finely chopped (optional)	1/4 c. vegetable oil

Place the freshly-grated potatoes on a double thickness of paper towels. Fold the towels around them and twist and squeeze until most of the moisture is extracted. In a large bowl, combine the potatoes, onions, peppers, flour, cream, egg, salt and pepper. Toss until well mixed. In a large frying pan, over medium heat, add the oil and cook until just heated. Put about 2 tablespoons of the potato mixture into the pan and press and shape with a spatula into a flat pancake. Repeat until the pan is full but not crowded. Cook each pancake about 5 minutes, until the bottom is crisp and brown. Turn and cook the other side another 5 minutes more. Place in a baking dish. Cover and keep warm in a 300° oven until all are done. Serve immediately.

SAUTEED ARTICHOKE HEARTS
(This is about as easy as it gets! The spices complement the artichokes well, making this a simple yet delicious dish. You may sprinkle a little extra parsley on top before serving, if desired.)

4 Tbsp. butter
2 (9 oz.) cans artichoke
 hearts (not marinated),
 drained and rinsed
2 cloves garlic, minced

2 Tbsp. parsley
1/2 tsp. oregano
1/2 tsp. salt
1/4 tsp. pepper

In a large frying pan, over medium heat, melt butter. Add all other ingredients. Cook 5 - 7 minutes, stirring occasionally. Remove from heat. Place in a serving dish and serve immediately.

THE HARRIED HOUSEWIFE SAYS....
 One of the best ways to entertain friends and family is to call them on the telephone at the last minute and see if they are free. Too much preparation can ruin a good thing!

VEGETABLES

SAUTEED ZUCCHINI

(This is so easy and tastes so good. A perfect vegetable for just about any dinner. You may sprinkle a little extra parsley on top before serving, if desired.)

2 Tbsp. olive oil	1/2 tsp. salt
1 large zucchini, cut	1/4 tsp. oregano
into thin slices	1/4 tsp. basil
2 cloves garlic, minced	1/4 tsp. pepper
1/2 tsp. parsley	

In a large frying pan, over medium heat, add olive oil and cook until just heated. Add all other ingredients. Cook until zucchini is tender, about 5 - 7 minutes, stirring occasionally. Remove from heat. Place in a serving dish and serve immediately.

SCALLOPED CORN

(The cayenne pepper in this dish offers just enough "bite" to add a distinct, delicious flavor. Of course, you can always add more or less to suit your taste.)

3 Tbsp. flour	1 small onion, finely chopped
1 tsp. salt	1 c. milk
1/2 tsp. paprika	2 cans corn, drained
1/4 tsp. cayenne pepper	1 egg yolk
3 Tbsp. butter	1 c. seasoned bread crumbs
1 small green pepper,	
finely chopped	

Preheat oven to 400°. Butter a 1 1/2 quart baking dish. In a medium bowl, mix together flour, salt, paprika and cayenne pepper. Set aside. In a large frying pan, over medium heat, melt butter. Add peppers and onions. Cook until soft, about 5 minutes.

Stir in the flour mixture. Cook, stirring constantly, 2 - 3 minutes. Add milk, still stirring, and bring to a boil. (You may have to increase the heat.) Remove from burner and add corn and egg yolk. Mix well. Spoon into prepared baking dish and sprinkle with bread crumbs. Bake 25 - 30 minutes, until the crumbs are brown. Serve immediately.

ZUCCHINI CASSEROLE
(This dish is a surefire winner! The delicate flavor of zucchini is strongly enhanced by the choice of Italian spices. For a change, you may omit the onions and add two cloves garlic, minced. Whichever way you choose, you are sure to enjoy.)

2 medium zucchini, thinly sliced	1 tsp. oregano
1/2 small onion, finely chopped	1/2 tsp. basil
	1/2 tsp. salt
3 eggs, slightly beaten	1/4 tsp. pepper
2 tsp. parsley	4 Tbsp. butter
	1 c. cracker crumbs

Preheat oven to 350°. Butter a 1 1/2 quart casserole. Boil zucchini for 3 minutes or until tender. Drain. Put into a large bowl and add onions, eggs, parsley, oregano, basil, salt and pepper. Mix until well blended. Pour into prepared casserole. In a small frying pan, over medium heat, melt butter. Add cracker crumbs and stir until well coated. Remove from heat and sprinkle over zucchini. Bake 35 - 40 minutes. Serve immediately.

MEATS, POULTRY, MAIN DISHES

MEATS, POULTRY, MAIN DISHES

BAKED FISH
(This is an easy way to prepare fish. You may use any kind of fish you prefer and may easily double the recipe. There is no need to turn fish while baking. Delicious!)

1 pound fish fillets	**1 tsp. onion powder**
1/2 tsp. salt	**1/4 c. mayonnaise**
1/4 tsp. white pepper	**1/4 tsp. paprika**

Preheat oven to 325°. Line 8" x 10" baking dish with foil. Place fish in pan. Sprinkle with salt, white pepper and onion powder. Coat the top of fillets with mayonnaise using a pastry brush (or back of a large spoon). Sprinkle with paprika. Bake 20 - 25 minutes. Serve immediately.

BARBECUED BEEF
(This is great because you can quickly prepare it, put it into the oven and forget about it for three hours! The tender beef, mixed with just the right amount of tangy ingredients, makes this a melt-in-your mouth pleasure!)

3 - 4 pound chuck roast	**2 Tbsp. wine vinegar**
1 medium onion,	**2 Tbsp. Worcestershire sauce**
coarsely chopped	**1 Tbsp. sugar**
1 c. ketchup	**2 tsp. salt**
1 c. water	**1/2 tsp. pepper**
1/2 c. sweet relish	

Preheat oven to 300°. Place roast in a baking pan. In a large bowl, mix together all other ingredients. Pour over roast. Cover and bake about 3 hours, until meat is tender enough to shred with a fork. Remove meat from pan. Cool and then shred it fine. Add to the juice and reheat in a 350° oven for 30 minutes. Serve on buns or rolls.

BARBECUED LONDON BROIL

(This london broil is tender and full-of-flavor. The can of beer adds to the taste. A delicious accompaniment might be Noodles Alfredo and the perfect vegetable, Sauteed Zucchini. Finish it off with Chocolate Dipped Strawberries and they'll love you forever!)

3 - 4 pound london broil
1 can beer
1/4 c. wine vinegar
1/4 c. olive oil

2 cloves garlic, minced
1/4 tsp. pepper
1 c. hickory-flavored barbecue
  sauce

Place london broil into a large bowl. In a separate, medium bowl, mix together all other ingredients except barbecue sauce. Pour mixture over london broil. Cover and marinate 6 - 8 hours or overnight. Grill on a medium fire about 20 minutes, basting with the barbecue sauce and turning frequently. Cut into thin slices. Serve immediately.

CHEESEBURGER CASSEROLE

(This is a meal in itself. Everything you need is in this one delicious casserole. The best part is, even children like it!)

2 Tbsp. vegetable oil
1 pound lean ground beef
1 medium onion, chopped
1 medium green pepper,
  chopped (optional)
1 c. tomato sauce
1 tsp. salt
1/4 tsp. pepper
2 eggs, beaten

2 cans corn, drained and
  divided
4 medium tomatoes, sliced and
  divided
4 slices American cheese,
  divided
1/2 c. corn flake crumbs
2 Tbsp. butter, cubed

Preheat oven to 350°. Lightly butter a 9" x 13" baking dish. In a large frying pan, over medium heat, add oil, ground beef, onions and peppers. Cook 3 minutes. Remove from heat and drain, if necessary. Add sauce, salt and pepper. Mix well. Stir in eggs. Place 1 can of corn in prepared baking dish. Layer half of meat mixture over. Place half of tomato slices over meat mixture and top with half of cheese. Repeat. Cover with corn flake crumbs and dot with butter. Cover and bake 45 minutes. Let stand 5 - 7 minutes before serving.

CHICKEN AND HAM BAKE
(This dish is so full-of-flavor, you will want to share it with everyone. What makes it especially appealing is the fact that it is a great way to use leftover ham and chicken. While this recipe calls for one cup heavy cream, you may find it is not necessary to use this much as you will only need enough to just cover chicken.)

6 Tbsp. butter
1 medium onion, thinly
  sliced
1 (8 oz.) pkg. fresh,
  sliced mushrooms
8 slices cooked ham,
  thinly sliced

8 slices cooked chicken breast,
  about 1/4" - 1/2" thickness
1 c. heavy cream
1/2 c. Parmesan cheese
1 Tbsp. paprika

Preheat oven to 350°. Lightly butter a 9" x 13" baking dish. In a medium frying pan, over medium heat, melt butter. Add onions and mushrooms. Cook 5 minutes, stirring frequently. Spread onion and mushroom mixture in prepared baking dish. Place ham slices on top. Place chicken slices on top of each ham slice. Pour cream until just covered. Sprinkle Parmesan cheese over all and top with paprika. Bake 25 - 30 minutes. Let stand 5 - 7 minutes before serving.

CHICKEN CASSEROLE

(This is another dish that can be prepared earlier in the day, placed in the oven to bake and forgotten about for three hours. Tender chicken with a delectable bacon slice wrapped around it smothered in a creamy sauce with just a touch of mushrooms make them swear you are a gourmet cook! A good accompaniment might be Linguine with Garlic and Oil and a freshly tossed salad along with a crusty, French bread. Most importantly, a glass of chilled chardonnay will complement this meal. Cheers!)

4 oz. dried beef	1/2 c. fresh mushrooms, sliced
8 slices bacon	1 can cream-of-mushroom
4 chicken breasts,	soup
skinless and boneless,	1 c. sour cream
halved (total 8 breasts)	1/4 tsp. paprika
1/4 tsp. pepper	

Preheat oven to 275°. Butter a 9" x 13" baking dish. Place dried beef on the bottom of prepared dish. Wrap a slice of bacon around each half of chicken breast. Place breasts on dried beef. Sprinkle pepper over. Place mushrooms on breasts. In a medium bowl, mix together soup and sour cream. Spread on mushrooms. Sprinkle paprika on top. Cover and bake 3 hours. Let stand 5 - 7 minutes before serving.

THE HARRIED HOUSEWIFE SAYS....
There is no reason to follow a recipe exactly. Improvise with whatever you happen to have and whatever appeals to you. Just think, you will have created a new recipe!

CHICKEN CITRUS TARRAGON
(A delicious, zesty dish enhanced by the combination of tangy juices and flavorful spices. Excellent choice for a backyard barbecue during summer months or may be broiled during winter months.)

4 chicken breasts,	1 tsp. parsley
skinless and boneless	1 tsp. tarragon
1/2 c. lemon juice	1/2 tsp. ginger
1/2 c. orange juice	1/2 tsp. salt
3 cloves garlic, minced	1/4 tsp. pepper
1 Tbsp. olive oil	

Place chicken into a large bowl. In a separate, medium bowl, mix together all other ingredients. Pour over chicken. Cover and marinate at least 2 hours. Grill on a medium fire about 25 - 30 minutes, basting frequently until 5 minutes before chicken is done. Serve immediately.

CHICKEN CORDON BLEU
(This dish always seemed like it would be difficult to prepare. I just associated it with ordering it in a restaurant, never thinking I could make it myself. This recipe is about as easy as it gets and tastes just as good, if not better, than what you might get in a restaurant. Just remember to remove the toothpicks before serving!)

4 chicken breasts,	1/2 tsp. thyme
skinless and boneless	1/4 tsp. nutmeg
4 slices ham, thinly	1/4 tsp. salt
sliced	1/4 tsp. pepper
5 oz. Swiss cheese,	1/4 c. white wine
sliced into 4 strips	1 1/2 c. chicken gravy
2 Tbsp. butter	
1 (8 oz.) pkg. fresh	
mushrooms, sliced	

Place chicken between two pieces of plastic wrap and pound to 1/4" thickness. Put 1 ham slice and 1 cheese strip on each breast. Roll chicken, jelly-roll style, tucking in ends and securing with toothpicks. In a large frying pan, over medium heat, melt butter and add chicken. Brown on both sides. Remove chicken. In the same frying pan, add mushrooms, thyme, nutmeg, salt and pepper. Cook 5 minutes, stirring occasionally. Stir in wine and gravy. Add chicken to frying pan and continue cooking, covered over medium-low heat, until chicken is done, about 15 minutes (turn once). Serve immediately.

CHICKEN, CREAMY PAPRIKA

(This tastes so good and you can whip it up in no time at all! The chicken is tender and the creamy sauce is heavenly. Seasoned Rice would go well with this as would hot, buttered green beans. This just re-enforces the fact that it doesn't take a lot of time or effort to put together a delicious, homemade meal. Enjoy!)

4 chicken breasts, skinless and boneless	1 c. mayonnaise
4 slices Muenster cheese	1 tsp. paprika
1 can cream-of-chicken soup	1 c. seasoned bread crumbs

Preheat oven to 350°. Place chicken in a 9" x 13" baking dish. Place 1 piece of cheese over each breast. In a medium bowl, mix together soup and mayonnaise. Pour soup mixture over breasts and sprinkle with paprika. Pour bread crumbs over all. Cover and bake 55 - 60 minutes, until chicken is tender. Let stand 5 - 7 minutes before serving.

CHICKEN DIJON

(The mustard in this dish adds a delicious, unique flavor. It is such an easy dish to prepare, just cook on top of the stove. This recipe doesn't call for too many ingredients, which certainly adds to the appeal.)

3 Tbsp. butter	1 c. water
4 chicken breasts,	1 tsp. chicken boullion
skinless and boneless	1/2 c. light cream
2 Tbsp. flour	2 Tbsp. Dijon mustard

In a large frying pan, over medium heat, melt butter. Add breasts and cook until done, about 20 minutes, turning occasionally. Remove chicken. Stir in flour. Add water, boullion and cream. Continue stirring until thickened. Stir in mustard. Add chicken. Cover and cook until heated through, about 10 minutes. Serve immediately.

CHICKEN FAJITAS

(A delicious change from the usual! These fajitas are so tasty, and so easy-to-make, they are an excellent choice for a casual get-together.)

4 chicken breasts,	1/4 tsp. pepper
skinless and boneless,	1/4 tsp. crushed red pepper
cut into strips	1 large onion, cut into strips
1/2 c. lime juice	1 large green pepper, cut into
1/4 c. olive oil,	strips
plus 1 Tbsp.	tortillas
1/2 tsp. salt	

Place chicken into a large bowl. In a separate, medium bowl, mix together lime juice, 1/4 cup olive oil, salt, pepper and red pepper.

Pour over chicken. Cover and marinate at least 2 hours. Remove chicken from bowl and discard marinade. In a large frying pan, over medium heat, add remaining 1 tablespoon olive oil and cook until just heated. Add marinated chicken and cook 3 - 4 minutes, stirring frequently, until just about done. Add onions and peppers and cook until just tender, about 3 - 4 minutes. Serve on tortillas.

CHICKEN FLORENTINE

(This is a favorite. If you really want to impress them, this is a good recipe to choose. It is easy-to-make and tastes just as good, if not better, than what you might order in an Italian restaurant. The side dish which usually accompanies this is angel-hair pasta tossed with butter and garnished with just a touch of parsley. You might add Sauteed Zucchini, fresh from the oven garlic bread and of course, a nicely chilled bottle of chardonnay or chablis. Who said you couldn't cook?!)

4 chicken breasts,
  skinless and boneless
6 Tbsp. butter, divided
1 (12 oz.) pkg. fresh
  mushrooms, sliced
2 c. flour
1/2 tsp. salt
1/4 tsp. pepper
4 eggs

1/2 pound bacon, coarsely
  chopped
1 small onion, coarsely
  chopped
2 cloves garlic, minced
1 (10 oz.) pkg. frozen, chopped
  spinach, thawed
1/2 c. white wine

Preheat oven to 350°. Pound chicken between two pieces of plastic wrap to 1/4" thickness. In a large frying pan, over medium heat, melt 3 tablespoons butter and add mushrooms. Cook 5 minutes. In a medium bowl, combine flour with salt and pepper. Set aside. In a separate, medium bowl, beat eggs. Dip chicken into eggs and then into flour mixture. Add the remaining butter to the same frying pan and, over medium heat, cook chicken until slightly brown on both sides, about 5 minutes. In a separate, large frying pan over medium heat, add bacon and cook until almost done, about 3 - 5 minutes. Drain fat, reserving about 1 teaspoonful. Add onions and garlic. Cook until just tender, about 3 - 5 minutes. Add spinach and wine. Cover and simmer 5 minutes more, stirring occasionally. In the bottom of a 9" x 13" baking dish, place spinach and bacon mixture. Top with chicken breasts and mushrooms. Sprinkle with parsley, if desired. Cover and bake 30 - 35 minutes. Serve immediately.

CHICKEN ITALIANO

(These bite-size pieces of tender chicken can be made ahead of time and served cold for a delicious snack or unique appetizer, or may be prepared for dinner. You may easily double this recipe as whichever way you choose to serve them, they won't last long!)

1/2 c. sour cream
1 egg
3/4 c. seasoned bread
 crumbs
1/3 c. Parmesan cheese
1 tsp. parsley

1/2 tsp. salt
1/4 tsp. pepper
2 chicken breasts, skinless and
 boneless, cut into bite-size
 pieces

Preheat oven to 350°. Lightly grease a 1 1/2 quart baking dish. In a small bowl, mix together sour cream and egg. In a separate, medium bowl, mix together bread crumbs, Parmesan cheese, parsley, salt and pepper. Dip each piece of chicken into sour cream mixture and then into bread crumb mixture, being sure to coat evenly. Place in prepared baking dish. Cover and bake 45 minutes. Serve hot or cold.

CHICKEN MARINADE

(This is your basic, simple marinade. The longer you marinate chicken, the better it will taste. While this chicken tastes great cooked on a grill, it may also be broiled or even baked in a 350° oven for about one hour. If you decide to bake it, you may want to scrub a few potatoes, pierce each one about three times with a fork, wrap each one in aluminum foil and place alongside chicken in oven to bake for one hour. All you need to do is add a vegetable and you have another easy, delicious meal!)

4 chicken breasts,   1/2 tsp. salt
  skinless and boneless   1/2 tsp. parsley
1/2 c. white wine   1/4 tsp. basil
1/4 c. olive oil   1/4 tsp. pepper
1 clove garlic, minced

Place chicken into a large bowl. In a separate, medium bowl, mix together all other ingredients. Pour over chicken. Cover and marinate at least 2 hours. Grill on a medium fire 20 - 25 minutes, basting frequently and turning occasionally. Stop basting 5 minutes before chicken is done. Serve immediately.

THE HARRIED HOUSEWIFE SAYS....
If you are worried you cannot invite certain people over to your house for fear they will pay more attention to your house and its surroundings than to you, ask yourself if you really want to spend time with these types of people!

CHICKEN RIGGIES

(The most popular dish of all! What makes this recipe so special is the fact that it is easy-to-make and is full-of-flavor. The chicken is tender and the olives add a surprisingly flavorful touch. Add a freshly tossed salad and warm garlic bread. Oh, and don't forget the most important thing to complement this tasty meal, a nicely chilled bottle of red wine. My personal favorite, Cabernet Sauvignon. Salute!)

4 Tbsp. butter
2 chicken breasts, skinless and boneless, cut into bite-size pieces
1 (8 oz.) pkg. fresh mushrooms, sliced
1 medium green pepper, coarsely chopped
1 medium onion, coarsely chopped
2 c. water

2 tsp. boullion (or 2 cubes)
1 c. tomato sauce
1/2 pt. heavy cream
1 tsp. paprika
1 tsp. parsley
1/2 tsp. salt
1/4 tsp. pepper
1/2 c. green (Spanish) olives
2 Tbsp. cornstarch
1 pound Rigatoni, cooked and drained

In a large pan, over medium heat, melt butter. Add chicken and cook until tender, about 5 - 7 minutes, stirring frequently. Add mushrooms and cook 5 minutes more. Add peppers and onions and continue cooking until soft, about 5 - 7 minutes. Add water, boullion, sauce, heavy cream, paprika, parsley, salt and pepper. Bring to a boil. Reduce heat, cover and simmer 20 minutes, stirring occasionally. Add olives and simmer 5 minutes more. In a small bowl, mix cornstarch with 2 tablespoons of water until it dissolves. Add to the sauce, stirring continuously until it thickens. When thickened, mix sauce and Rigatoni together in a deep bowl. Serve immediately. May sprinkle Parmesan cheese on top, if desired.

Tip: *If you are going to use skinless, boneless chicken breasts in a recipe and they have to be cut, they will be easier to cut if they are partially frozen.*

CHICKEN, SWEET AND SOUR

(Serve this tasty dish over rice. The combination of sweet and sour is perfect. The pineapples and brown sugar add just the right amount of sweetness while the wine vinegar and soy sauce add their own unique flavor. With just a hint of ginger, this recipe is sure to please.)

2 Tbsp. olive oil
2 chicken breasts,
  skinless and boneless,
  cut into bite-size pieces
1 medium green pepper,
  cut into strips
1 medium red pepper,
  cut into strips
1 medium carrot,
  peeled and cut into strips

1 clove garlic, minced
1 (8 oz.) can chunk pineapple
  in juice
3 Tbsp. wine vinegar
3 Tbsp. brown sugar
1/2 tsp. ginger
1 Tbsp. cornstarch
1/4 c. soy sauce

In a large frying pan, over medium heat, add oil. Cook until just heated. Add chicken and brown on all sides. Add peppers, carrots and garlic. Cook, stirring constantly, 2 minutes. Add pineapples and juice, vinegar, brown sugar and ginger. Cook 2 minutes more, stirring continuously. In a small bowl, mix together cornstarch with soy sauce until it dissolves. Add to the pan, stirring constantly, until it thickens. When thickened, remove from heat. Serve immediately over rice.

Tip: When a recipe calls for rice, always try to make extra as you can always use whatever is leftover in soups or even heated on the stove with a little water, boullion, soy sauce and mixed vegetables.

CHICKEN TENDERS

(This is about as easy as it gets! Delicious, tender pieces of bite-size chicken that can be made ahead of time and served cold for a delicious appetizer or may be prepared for dinner. You may easily double this recipe as it is sure to be a favorite!)

2 chicken breasts,
  skinless and boneless,
  cut into bite-size pieces
1/2 c. mayonnaise

3/4 c. seasoned bread crumbs
1/4 c. Parmesan cheese
1/2 tsp. salt
1/4 tsp. pepper

Preheat oven to 350°. Lightly grease a 1 1/2 quart casserole. Place chicken into a large bowl. Add mayonnaise and gently toss. In a separate, medium bowl, mix together all other ingredients. Add this mixture to the chicken mixture and gently stir, being sure to coat each piece of chicken with the bread crumbs. Put into prepared casserole. Cover and bake 45 minutes. Serve hot or cold.

CHICKEN TERIYAKI WITH LEMON

(This dish is simple and delicious. The combination of ingredients, particularly lemon juice, adds a distinctive flavor. There is plenty of garlic but you may adjust the amount to your own taste without sacrificing the flavor. Serve over rice.)

1/2 c. lemon juice
1/2 c. soy sauce
1/4 c. sugar
2 Tbsp. water

4 cloves garlic, minced
3/4 tsp. ginger
8 chicken thighs, skinless

In a large frying pan, over medium heat, add all ingredients except chicken. Cook, stirring frequently, 3 - 4 minutes. Add chicken. Reduce heat. Cover and simmer, stirring occasionally, 25 minutes or until chicken is tender. Serve over rice.

CHILI CON CARNE

(Nothing seems to warm you up as quickly after being outside in the cold as much as a good, thick, hearty bowl of chili. And nothing seems to compare to the smell wafting through the air as you walk through the door. On cold, winter days my father always says, "It's a great day for chili." He's right.)

1 (16 oz.) can kidney beans, undrained	1 pound lean ground beef
1/2 tsp. salt	1 (28 oz.) can tomatoes, coarsely chopped
4 Tbsp. olive oil	1 c. tomato sauce
1 small onion, coarsely chopped	1 tsp. chili powder
1 small green pepper, coarsely chopped	1/2 tsp. ground red pepper (more or less, as desired)
2 cloves garlic, minced	1/4 tsp. pepper

In a small pan, over low heat, add kidney beans and salt. Cover and cook 30 minutes, stirring occasionally. In a large pan, over medium heat, add oil, onions, peppers and garlic. Cook 5 minutes, stirring occasionally. Add ground beef and cook until browned. Drain, if necessary. Add kidney beans, chopped tomatoes and their juice, tomato sauce, chili powder, ground red pepper and pepper. Bring to a boil. Reduce heat. Cover and simmer 50 - 55 minutes, stirring occasionally. Serve immediately. Tastes even better the next day!

Tip: *Cut up some hard cheese such as Cheddar and add to your bowl of chili. Delicious!*

CHILI DOGS

(This is another easy-to-make dish requiring little or no preparation as you probably already have all the ingredients in the kitchen. The best part of this recipe is that you can decide to make it at the last minute and it tastes as if you spent all day making chili just for them!)

1 Tbsp. olive oil
1/2 small onion,
  finely chopped
1 clove garlic, minced
1/2 pound lean ground
  beef
2 c. tomato sauce

1/2 tsp. chili powder
1/2 tsp. salt
1/8 tsp. ground red pepper
  (more or less, as desired)
8 hot dogs
8 hot dog rolls

In a large frying pan, over medium heat, add olive oil, onions and garlic. Cook 2 - 3 minutes. Add ground beef and cook until browned. Drain, if necessary. Add tomato sauce, chili powder, salt and ground red pepper. Bring to a boil. Reduce heat. Cover and simmer 10 - 15 minutes. In a separate pan, cook hot dogs as desired. Place hot dogs in rolls and spoon chili over. For a delicious change, top chili dogs with shredded cheese. Whatever you happen to have will taste great!

THE HARRIED HOUSEWIFE SAYS....
A sense-of-humor in everyday living is about as important to a happy lifestyle as ground red pepper is to a bowl of chili!

CHIPPED BEEF GRAVY

(This recipe has been in the family for many years. The old-fashioned, homemade flavor is uncompromising. Serve over toast, potatoes or rice. My grandmother used to enjoy it over steamed cauliflower. Whichever way you choose, this classic taste is always a favorite.)

6 oz. dried beef	1/2 c. heavy cream
4 Tbsp. butter	1/2 tsp. pepper
4 Tbsp. flour	1/2 tsp. dry mustard
1 c. milk (heated)	1/4 tsp. ginger

Cover dried beef with boiling water. Let stand 5 minutes. Drain and cut into small pieces. In a medium pan, melt butter over medium-high heat. Add flour and cook until light golden color, stirring continuously. Stir in hot milk. When thickened, add cream and seasonings. Stir until smooth. Reduce heat and simmer 5 minutes more, stirring often. Add beef and stir to mix. Serve as you like, over toast, potatoes or rice.

CREAMY MACARONI AND CHEESE

(This delicious dish has a creamy, smooth texture with a slightly different flavor than the usual macaroni and cheese dishes we have grown accustomed to. The addition of cottage cheese and sour cream make this unique casserole a delightful change. You can easily double this recipe for a larger crowd or cut it in half for just the two of you. Enjoy!)

2 c. cottage cheese, small curd	1 c. sharp Cheddar cheese, grated
1 c. sour cream	1 c. elbow macaroni, cooked
1 egg, slightly beaten	and drained
1/2 tsp. salt	1/4 tsp. paprika
1/4 tsp. pepper	

Preheat oven to 350°. Lightly butter a 2 quart casserole. In a large bowl, mix together cottage cheese, sour cream, egg, salt and pepper. Add cheese and mix well. Add macaroni and gently stir to mix well. Pour into prepared casserole. Sprinkle paprika on top. Cover and bake 45 minutes. Let stand 5 - 7 minutes before serving.

CREAMY NOODLE CASSEROLE

(This is another easy casserole that is full-of-flavor. Sometimes when I am in a hurry I just boil egg noodles, drain and add a little butter to lightly coat and serve with whatever chicken or meat dish we are having. It is a good idea to make extra egg noodles and refrigerate them to use the next day in this recipe. You will be saving time and it will taste great!)

1 1/4 c. cottage cheese, small curd	1 egg, slightly beaten
1 c. sour cream	1/2 tsp. parsley
1/2 c. egg noodles, cooked and drained	1/2 tsp. salt
	1/4 tsp. pepper
	3/4 c. corn flakes, crushed

Preheat oven to 350°. Lightly butter a 1 1/2 casserole. In a medium bowl, combine all ingredients except corn flakes. Gently stir to mix. Pour into prepared casserole and sprinkle crumbs on top. Cover and bake 1 hour. Let stand 5 - 7 minutes before serving.

THE HARRIED HOUSEWIFE SAYS....
The beauty of creating your own recipe with whatever you happen to have in the house is that it is truly a unique work-of-art. Unfortunately, if you are like me, you will forget how to create your unique "work-of-art" again unless you immediately write it down!

CROCK POT BEEF

(It doesn't get any easier than this! Put everything in the crock pot in the morning and forget about it! It cooks for eight hours, freeing you up for the day. Just serve on buns or my favorite way is over the top of warm garlic bread. Add a freshly tossed salad and you're all set!)

4 - 5 pound roast,
 coarsely chopped
3 tsp. beef boullion

1 clove garlic, minced
2 Tbsp. Italian salad dressing

Place roast in crock pot. Add all other ingredients and enough water to cover beef. Cook on low 8 hours. With a knife and fork, shred beef (can leave beef in the crock pot to do this). Serve on buns or garlic bread, as desired.

CROCK POT CABBAGE ROLLS

(Another delicious, easy meal! These are so good, they won't last long! What would we do without crock pots?!)

12 large cabbage leaves
1 pound lean ground
 beef
1 c. rice, cooked
1 egg, beaten
1/4 c. milk
1/4 c. onions, finely
 chopped

1 tsp. salt
1/4 tsp. pepper
1 c. tomato sauce
1 Tbsp. brown sugar
1 Tbsp. lemon juice
1 tsp. Worcestershire sauce

In a large pan, boil water and add cabbage leaves. Cook until limp, about 3 minutes. Drain. In a large bowl, combine ground beef, rice, egg, mik, onions, salt and pepper. Mix well (freshly washed hands work best!). Place about 1/4 cup meat mixture in center of each leaf. Fold in sides and roll ends over meat. Place in crock pot. In a small bowl, combine sauce, brown sugar, lemon juice and Worcestershire sauce. Mix well. Pour over cabbage rolls. Cover and cook on low 8 hours.

GOULASH

(This recipe has been around for years. My mother used to make it all the time for us when we were little because it tasted good and was very inexpensive to make. Of course she always doubled it as there was always a few extra kids at our house! You will certainly get your money's worth from this recipe.)

1/2 pound lean ground
  beef
1 clove garlic, minced
1 (28 oz.) can tomatoes,
  coarsely chopped
1 c. tomato sauce
1/2 c. water
1/2 tsp. beef boullion

1/2 tsp. parsley
1/2 tsp. salt
1/4 tsp. oregano
1/4 tsp. pepper
1 c. elbow macaroni,
  cooked and drained
1 Tbsp. butter

In a large pan, over medium, add ground beef and garlic. Cook until beef has browned. Drain, if necessary. Add chopped tomatoes and their juice, sauce, water, boullion and spices. Bring to a boil. Reduce heat, cover and simmer 10 minutes, stirring occasionally. Add macaroni to beef and tomato mixture and gently stir. Add butter and continue to cook over medium-low heat until thoroughly heated, about 5 minutes. Remove from heat. Cover and let stand 5 minutes before serving.

THE HARRIED HOUSEWIFE SAYS:
Did you ever notice that even though you may have the very same thing at your house, even if it's a peanut butter and jelly sandwich, it always tastes better at someone else's house!

GREEKBURGERS
(These are an absolute favorite! Another most requested recipe! They have just enough spice to make them uniquely delicious! The addition of wine, olive oil and mustard lend their own unique touch. Mixed altogether, these are delicious! Serve on a lettuce leaf or bun.)

1 - 1 1/2 pounds lean
  ground beef
1/4 c. red wine
1/4 c. olive oil
2 cloves garlic, minced

1 tsp. mustard
1 tsp. oregano
1/2 tsp. salt
1/4 tsp. pepper

In a large bowl, add all ingredients and mix well. Shape into patties. Grill over a medium fire, as desired, about 5 minutes on each side. Serve immediately.

GRILLED VEGETABLE KABOBS WITH RICE
(These are just about the tastiest kabobs you will ever have! The combination of Italian salad dressing, parsley and basil add a lively flavor to fresh vegetables. Of course you may substitute any kind of vegetables you choose, depending on whatever is in season and your personal preference. A delicious dish to enjoy with these might be Chicken Citrus Tarragon. A nice glass of chilled white wine such as chablis will certainly complement this meal.)

1/2 c. Italian salad dressing
1 tsp. parsley
1 tsp. basil
2 medium yellow squash,
  cut into 1" slices
8 small boiling onions

8 cherry tomatoes
8 medium fresh mushrooms,
  stems removed
vegetable cooking spray
2 c. rice, cooked

In a small bowl, combine dressing, parsley and basil. Cover and chill. On 8 skewers alternate, squash, onions, tomatoes and mushrooms. Coat grill rack with cooking spray. Over medium-high fire, cook kabobs 15 - 20 minutes or until vegetables are tender, turning and basting frequently with dressing mixture. To serve, place about 1/2 cup of rice on each plate and top with 2 vegetable kabobs.

HAM AND CHEESE STRATA

(This dish is best prepared in the morning as it needs to be refrigerated six to eight hours before baking. Put it in the oven to bake for about one hour and you're all set. Everything is already in it. This tastes delicious and is filled with true, homemade flavor.)

12 slices white bread,
  crusts removed
1 1/2 c. Mozzarella
  cheese, shredded
1 c. cooked ham,
  coarsely chopped
1 c. cooked broccoli,
  coarsely chopped

1/4 c. onions, finely chopped
8 eggs
3 c. milk
2 Tbsp. salsa, hot, medium or
  mild
1/2 tsp. salt
1/4 tsp. pepper

Lightly butter a 9" x 13" baking dish. Line the bottom with 6 bread slices; top with half the cheese, half the ham and half the broccoli and onions. Add another layer of bread slices and top with remaining cheese, ham, broccoli and onions. In a medium bowl, mix together the eggs, milk, salsa, salt and pepper. Pour mixture over bread and cheese layers. With a fork, pierce through all layers in 6 places, then press bread down into egg mixture until it is covered. Cover and refrigerate 6 - 8 hours. Bake, uncovered, in a 350° oven 55 - 60 minutes. Let stand 5 - 7 minutes before serving.

HAMBURGER CASSEROLE

(This is a delicious, inexpensive meal in itself. It's great for a larger crowd or can be easily halved. While this casserole needs to stand 5 - 10 minutes before serving, you may want to prepare Biscuits while the casserole is baking, take casserole out of the oven and increase the temperature to 375°, pop Biscuits into the oven to bake while casserole is standing. They will both be ready to serve at the same time and nothing tastes better than freshly baked Biscuits!)

1 pound lean ground
  beef
1 medium onion,
  chopped
2 c. tomato sauce
1/2 tsp. salt
1/4 tsp. pepper
1 c. cottage cheese,
  small curd

1 (8 oz.) pkg. cream cheese,
  softened
1/4 c. sour cream
1/2 small green pepper,
  chopped
1 c. egg noodles, cooked and
  drained

Preheat oven to 350°. In a large frying pan, over medium heat, add ground beef and onions. Cook until ground beef has browned. Drain, if necessary. Stir in sauce, salt and pepper. Cover and simmer 5 minutes, stirring occasionally. In a medium bowl, mix together cottage cheese, cream cheese, sour cream and green peppers. Gently stir in egg noodles. In a 3 quart casserole, spread noodle mixture on the bottom and ground beef mixture on top. Cover and bake 45 minutes. Let stand 5 - 10 minutes before serving.

KIELBASA CASSEROLE

(This is another tasty, inexpensive meal in itself. While this recipe calls for using a 9" x 13" baking dish, if your family is not this large, you may split this recipe in half using two baking dishes or casseroles. Bake one now and freeze one for later. This doesn't usually last long at my house! Enjoy!)

1 - 1 1/2 pounds polish
  Kielbasa, coarsely
  chopped
1 small cabbage, cored
  and sliced
3 medium potatoes,
  peeled and sliced
1/4 c. water
1 large onion, sliced

1 large green pepper, sliced
3 medium carrots, peeled,
  halved and sliced
1 c. tomato sauce
1 tsp. parsley
1/2 tsp. salt
1/4 tsp. pepper
2 Tbsp. butter, cubed

Preheat oven to 350°. Lightly butter a 9" x 13" baking dish. Arrange ingredients in baking dish in order given, topping with tomato sauce, parsley, salt and pepper and dotting with butter. Cover and bake 1 hour. Let stand 5 - 10 minutes before serving.

THE HARRIED HOUSEWIFE SAYS....
  One of the secrets of successful entertaining is choosing as many recipes as possible which can be prepared early in the day and refrigerated until ready to use. This frees you up to pay attention to the little details you might not have otherwise noticed. Believe me, it took me a long time to figure this out!

LASAGNE FLORENTINE

(This is one of my all-time favorite recipes. Of course, I happen to love spinach and this dish is filled with just the right amount of spinach mixed with three different cheeses and just the right amount of garlic and seasonings. Add a loaf of fresh Italian bread and a freshly tossed salad or antipasto and you're all set!)

1 Tbsp. olive oil
1 small onion, finely
  chopped
2 cloves garlic, minced
1 (10 oz.) pkg. frozen
  chopped spinach,
  thawed and drained
1 (16 oz.) container
  Ricotta cheese
1 c. Mozzarella cheese,
  shredded

1/2 c. Parmesan cheese
2 eggs, slightly beaten
2 Tbsp. parsley
1/2 tsp. salt
1/4 tsp. pepper
6 c. tomato sauce
12 lasagne noodles, cooked and
  drained

Preheat oven to 350°. In a small frying pan, over medium heat, add olive oil, onions and garlic. Cook until soft, about 5 minutes. In a large bowl, combine spinach, Ricotta cheese, Mozzarella cheese, Parmesan cheese, eggs, parsley, salt and pepper. Mix well. Add onion mixture and mix well. Spread 1/4 cup of tomato sauce in bottom of a 9" x 13" baking dish and cover with 3 lasagne noodles. Top with 1 cup of sauce. Cover with 1/3 spinach and cheese mixture, 1/3 sauce. Repeat layers 3 times, reserving about 1/4 cup sauce for the top. May sprinkle a little extra Parmesan cheese on top, if desired. Cover with foil and bake 50 - 55 minutes. Let stand 8 - 10 minutes before serving. Cut into squares.

LINGUINE WITH GARLIC AND OIL

(This dish is so easy to make and tastes so good. It goes well with just about any meat or poultry or can be enjoyed by itself with a freshly tossed salad and fresh Italian bread. Whichever way you choose, you will find it so tasty, you will be making it again and again.)

1 (12 oz.) pkg. fresh linguine	1 Tbsp. parsley
1/4 c. olive oil	1 tsp. salt
3 cloves garlic,	1/4 tsp. oregano
minced	1/4 tsp. pepper
	1 Tbsp. butter

In a large pan, boil 3 quarts of water, adding salt and oil, if desired. Add linguine and cook 3 - 4 minutes, stirring often. Cover and remove from heat. In a small frying pan, over medium-low heat, add olive oil and cook until just heated. Add garlic, parsley, salt, oregano and pepper. Cook 3 - 4 minutes, stirring often, being certain not to burn the garlic. Add butter and turn off heat. Drain linguine and return to the same pan. Add garlic and oil mixture and heat over medium-low, tossing well. When thoroughly heated, about 2 - 3 minutes, put into a large serving bowl. Sprinkle with extra parsley, if desired. Serve immediately.

THE HARRIED HOUSEWIFE SAYS....
You will know you have "arrived" when one of your guests wonders how you ever managed to find the time to prepare such an exquisite meal! (And kept the kitchen clean, to boot!)

LONDON BROIL TERIYAKI

(This tangy, tender, delicious london broil can be either grilled or broiled. It should be marinated 12 - 24 hours to derive the fullest flavor. A nice accompaniment might be Seasoned Rice and for a vegetable, perhaps Broiled Tomatoes with Cheese. You are sure to enjoy this flavorful dish!)

2 cloves garlic, minced	1/2 c. wine vinegar
1 tsp. ginger	3/4 c. water
1/4 c. brown sugar	1 Tbsp. cornstarch
1/4 c. ketchup	1 - 1 1/2 pounds london broil

In a medium pan, over medium heat, combine garlic, ginger, brown sugar, ketchup, vinegar and water. Cover and simmer 25 minutes, stirring occasionally. In a small bowl, dissolve cornstarch with 2 tablespoons of water. Add to the sauce. Stir continuously until sauce thickens. Remove from heat and cool. When cool, put london broil in a medium bowl and cover with sauce. Cover and marinate 12 - 24 hours. When ready to cook, drain and discard sauce and grill london broil over a medium fire for about 15 - 20 minutes, turning once. Slice thin and serve.

MEATBALLS

(These are about as easy and delicious as anyone could ever ask for! Of course, if you are having a larger crowd over for dinner, you may easily double this recipe. It is also a good idea to make extra and freeze them to add to sauce at a later date. Either way, enjoy these tasty meatballs!)

1/2 pound lean ground beef	2 eggs, lightly beaten
1/2 pound ground pork	1 tsp. garlic powder
1/2 c. seasoned bread crumbs	1/2 tsp. salt
1/4 c. Parmesan cheese	1/4 tsp. pepper
	2 Tbsp. olive oil

In a medium bowl, combine all ingredients except olive oil. Shape into balls, 1 1/2" in diameter (freshly washed hands work best!). In a large frying pan, heat the oil over medium heat and add meatballs, turning occasionally to brown on all sides. Add to spaghetti sauce, if desired, and simmer 20 minutes.

MEATLOAF
(Again, it is hard to believe how easy this is to make and how delicious it tastes! This meatloaf is tender and is not filled with so many ingredients that they wonder what is in it! It just emphasizes the point that a lot of times, less is always more. You do not need to add so many different ingredients to a recipe to make it taste good. This is a classic example.)

1 1/4 pounds lean ground beef	2 eggs, lightly beaten
3/4 pound ground pork	2 tsp. garlic powder
1 1/2 c. seasoned bread crumbs	1 tsp. onion powder
	1 tsp. salt
	1/2 tsp. pepper

Preheat oven to 350°. In a large bowl, combine all ingredients. Mix well (freshly washed hands work best!). Pat into a loaf pan and bake 50 - 60 minutes. Let stand 5 - 7 minutes before removing from pan and slicing. Serve immediately.

NOODLES ALFREDO

(These delicious, rich noodles are a cinch to make and everyone will think you went out of your way! They will never know the truth! The best part is, you won't have to hunt around the store for a certain, special ingredient because chances are, you already have most of what you need in the kitchen! This is the way to cook!)

1 c. wide egg noodles	1 c. Parmesan cheese
6 Tbsp. butter, melted	1/2 tsp. parsley
1 c. heavy cream,	1/2 tsp. salt
warmed	1/4 tsp. pepper

Cook noodles according to package directions. Drain and put into a medium serving bowl. Add remaining ingredients, tossing quickly to coat all noodles. May sprinkle with extra parsley, if desired. Serve at once.

PORK BARBECUE

(This simple, tasty dish is just what we need on those days when we absolutely do not feel like cooking! Mix everything together, pour over pork and forget about it for three hours. Add some hot, buttered noodles and a vegetable and you're all set! The tender meat is absolutely delicious. Enjoy!)

2 - 3 pounds pork	2 Tbsp. Worcestershire sauce
1/2 small onion,	2 Tbsp. wine vinegar
coarsely chopped	1 Tbsp. sugar
1 c. ketchup	1 tsp. salt
1 c. water	1/2 tsp. pepper

Preheat oven to 300°. Place pork in a 1 1/2 quart baking dish. In a medium bowl, mix together all other ingredients and pour over pork. Cover and bake about 3 hours, until meat is tender enough to shred with a fork. Remove meat and cool. Shred it fine. Add to the juice and reheat in a 350° oven for 30 minutes. Serve on buns.

PORK AND TOMATO BAKE

(Tender pork covered with a thick, delicious tomato sauce with just the right amount of garlic and spices. Excellent with Linguine with Garlic and Oil and Sauteed Zucchini. This is so easy to make and tastes so good!)

1 Tbsp. olive oil	1 Tbsp. parsley
4 - 5 center cut,	1/2 tsp. oregano
boneless pork chops	1/2 tsp. basil
1 (28 oz.) can tomatoes,	1/2 tsp. sugar
coarsely chopped	1/2 tsp. salt
2 cloves garlic,	1/4 tsp. pepper
minced	

Preheat oven to 350°. In a large frying pan, over medium heat, add olive oil and pork chops. Brown on both sides. Drain and put into a 9" x 13" baking dish. In a medium bowl, mix together tomatoes and their juice and all other ingredients. Pour over pork chops. Cover and bake 1 hour. Let stand 5 - 7 minutes before serving.

QUICHE, SPINACH AND BACON

(This is a quick, easy and delicious meal in itself. Even people who are not too fond of spinach will like this tasty dish as it is filled with flavor.)

8 slices cooked bacon,	1 c. sharp Cheddar cheese,
crumbled	cubed
1 (10 oz.) pkg. frozen,	4 eggs, lightly beaten
chopped spinach,	4 Tbsp. flour
thawed and drained	2 Tbsp. butter, cubed
1 c. cottage cheese,	
small curd	

Preheat oven to 350°. Lightly butter a 1 1/2 quart casserole. In a large bowl, mix together all ingredients. Pour into prepared casserole. Cover and bake 1 hour. Let stand 5 - 10 minutes before serving.

ROAST BEEF

(There are few greater pleasures than a simple meal of tender, juicy roast beef with mashed potatoes and gravy and hot, buttered vegetables. A meal such as this doesn't take much time to prepare and nothing says "homemade" better than this.)

4 pound eye-of-round
  beef
1 can cream-of-mushroom
  soup
1 envelope onion soup
  mix
1/2 small onion, finely
  chopped

3 cloves garlic, minced
1 c. red wine
1 c. water
1 tsp. thyme
1 tsp. parsley
1/2 tsp. pepper

Preheat oven to 350°. Place roast in a 3 quart casserole. In a large bowl, mix together all ingredients. Pour over beef. Cover and bake 3 1/2 - 4 hours, until beef is tender. Let stand 10 minutes before removing and slicing.

THE HARRIED HOUSEWIFE SAYS....
Sow the seeds of love into your children and you shall reap a bountiful harvest.

SCALLOPED POTATOES AND HAM

(This is another simple, old-fashioned recipe that always tastes good. It's a great way to use leftover ham and can be easily doubled if you have a larger crowd. Again, it seems the easiest recipes to make are often the ones that taste the best. This particular recipe just re-emphasizes the fact that too many ingredients and too many steps to follow are not necessary for a delicious, homemade dish.)

4 medium potatoes, peeled and sliced 1/4" thick	1/2 tsp. salt
	1/4 tsp. pepper
	3 Tbsp. flour
1 c. cooked ham, cubed	3 Tbsp. butter plus 1 Tbsp. butter
1/2 small onion, finely chopped	1 1/2 c. milk

Preheat oven to 350°. Butter a 1 1/2 quart casserole. Cover the bottom of casserole with a single layer of potatoes, then about 1/3 cup ham and about 1 tablespoon onions. Sprinkle with a little salt, pepper, 1 tablespoon flour and a few dots of butter. Repeat layers 2 times, until all potatoes, ham, onions, salt, pepper, flour and 3 tablespoons of butter are used. Pour milk over potato slices until the top is almost covered. Dot with the remaining 1 tablespoon of butter. Cover and bake 1 hour or until potatoes are tender. Let stand 8 - 10 minutes before serving.

SEAFOOD LASAGNE

(For those of us who enjoy seafood but don't particularly care for spending a lot of time preparing it, this is a dish we can really appreciate! It tastes as if hours were spent working on it when in reality it's so easy to quickly put together! This is definitely the way to do things!)

3 Tbsp. butter
2 cloves garlic, minced
3 Tbsp. flour
1/2 tsp. oregano
1/2 tsp. basil
1/2 tsp. parsley
1/4 tsp. pepper
1 c. milk
1 c. water
1 tsp. boullion

1 (10 oz.) pkg. frozen, cooked shrimp, thawed and rinsed
1/2 pound cooked crabmeat or imitation crab
1 c. Ricotta cheese
2 tsp. grated lemon peel
1 Tbsp. lemon juice
6 lasagne noodles, cooked, drained and cut in half
1/2 c. Parmesan cheese

Preheat oven to 375°. In a medium saucepan, over medium heat, add butter and garlic and cook 1 minute. Remove from heat. Stir in flour and seasonings until smooth. Gradually stir in milk, water and boullion until smooth. Bring to a boil, stirring continuously. Boil and stir 1 minute. Remove from heat. Gently stir in shrimp and crabmeat. In a separate, medium bowl, mix together Ricotta cheese, lemon peel and lemon juice. Into either a 8" or 9" square pan, spread about 1/2 cup sauce mixture. Layer 3 noodles over sauce. Top with about 1/3 Ricotta cheese mixture, 1/3 sauce mixture and 1/3 Parmesan cheese. Repeat layers of lasagne noodles, Ricotta cheese mixture and Parmesan cheese. Top with remaining lasagne noodles, sauce mixture and sprinkle with remaining Parmesan cheese. Cover with foil and bake 45 minutes. Let stand 8 - 10 minutes before cutting into squares.

SEASONED RICE

(This is another easy-to-make dish that you can make in a hurry and goes with just about anything. You may substitute beef boullion in place of chicken boullion for a different flavor, depending on whatever you happen to have.)

1 1/2 c. long-grain	3 tsp. chicken boullion
white rice	1 tsp. parsley
3 c. cold water	1 tsp. dried, minced onion

In a medium saucepan, over medium heat, add all ingredients and bring to a boil. Reduce heat, cover and simmer 20 minutes, without stirring. Remove from heat and let stand 5 minutes before serving.

SHRIMP CASSEROLE

(This is a delicious way to enjoy shrimp. The ground red pepper adds just enough flavor without being too overpowering. Of course, you may add more or less to suit your taste without sacrificing the flavor of the dish. Add a fresh garden salad and you're all set!)

2 Tbsp. butter	2 cans cream-of-shrimp soup
1/2 c. celery, chopped	1/4 c. dry sherry
1/2 small, green pepper,	1/4 c. sliced almonds, toasted
chopped	(optional)
2 - 3 c. shrimp, cleaned	1/2 tsp. salt
and cooked	1/8 tsp. ground red pepper
2 c. rice, cooked	1/4 tsp. paprika

Preheat oven to 350°. Lightly butter a 2 quart casserole. In a medium frying pan, over medium heat, add butter, celery and green peppers. Cook until soft, about 4 - 5 minutes. In a large bowl, add all other ingredients except paprika and mix well. Add celery and green pepper mixture. Mix well. Pour into prepared casserole. Sprinkle with paprika. Cover and bake 30 - 35 minutes. Serve immediately.

SHRIMP SCAMPI

*(This delicious dish is easy-to-make and tastes so good, you'll
wonder why you don't make it more often! You may buy shrimp
already peeled and deveined which will cost a little more but is
definitely worth it. Enjoy!)*

8 Tbsp. butter	3 cloves garlic, minced
2 pounds shrimp,	1 tsp. salt
peeled and deveined	1/4 tsp. pepper
1/2 small onion,	2 Tbsp. lemon juice
finely chopped	1 Tbsp. parsley

In a large frying pan, over medium heat, add butter, shrimp, onions
and garlic. Cook 5 minutes, turning shrimp once. Remove shrimp
and place on a hot serving dish. Set aside. Add salt, pepper and
lemon juice to the frying pan and cook 3 - 4 minutes more, stirring
continuously. Pour over shrimp and sprinkle with parsley. Serve
immediately.

SLOPPY JOES

*(This is another dish everyone loves. The best part is you can
decide to make it at the last minute as you probably already have
all the ingredients in your kitchen. Serve on buns, rolls or whatever
you happen to have. This is the way to cook!)*

1 pound lean	1 c. tomato sauce
ground beef	2 Tbsp. mustard
1/2 small onion,	1 Tbsp. wine vinegar
finely chopped	1/2 tsp. sugar
1/2 small green	1/2 tsp. salt
pepper, finely chopped	1/4 tsp. pepper

In a large frying pan, over medium heat, add ground beef, onions
and peppers and cook until beef has browned. Drain, if necessary.
Add all other ingedients. Cover and simmer 10 minutes. Serve hot.

SPAGHETTI SAUCE

(This is your basic, easy-to-make tomato sauce which you may use for whatever kind of pasta you choose. Of course, you can go that extra mile and make sauce from fresh, whole tomatoes and that would be really nice but realistically, who is going to do that everytime?! You may fry sausage in a separate frying pan and add to the sauce while it is simmering or add Meatballs. Actually, adding both and simmering together in the sauce is the best!)

1 (28 oz.) can tomatoes, coarsely chopped then mashed	1 clove garlic, minced
	1/2 tsp. sugar
	1/2 tsp. basil
1 (6 oz.) can tomato paste	1/2 tsp. oregano
1/2 c. water (or 1/2 c. red wine)	1/4 tsp. salt
	1/4 tsp. pepper
1 tsp. chicken boullion	1 Tbsp. butter

In a large pan, over medium heat, add tomatoes and their juice and all other ingredients except butter. Bring to a boil. Reduce heat, cover and simmer 45 minutes, stirring occasionally. Add butter and stir. Serve immediately over cooked pasta.

THE HARRIED HOUSEWIFE SAYS....
Isn't it funny how we suddenly have a resurgence of energy to clean our houses and organize everything after visiting a friend who always "appears" to have everything completely under control and is perfect in every way!

STUFFED SPINACH PIZZA

(This delightful, different pizza is so full-of-flavor you won't mind the little time it takes to roll out the dough. Of course, you may easily pat the first layer of dough into the pan, if desired and just roll the dough for the top layer. This little inconvenience is well worth it. You may also buy pizza dough already made (one pound bag) and this is great too. Whatever you happen to have will work!)

1 loaf (1 pound) frozen white bread dough	1/4 tsp. pepper
1 1/2 c. tomatoes, chopped	2 c. Ricotta cheese
3/4 pound loose Italian sausage, hot, medium or mild, cooked and drained	5 oz. (1/2 of 10 oz. pkg.) frozen, chopped spinach, thawed and and drained
1 tsp. basil	1 c. Mozzarella cheese, shredded
1/2 tsp. oregano	3/4 c. Parmesan cheese plus 1/4 c. (to sprinkle on top)
1/2 tsp. salt	2 cloves garlic, minced
	3/4 c. pizza sauce

Thaw bread dough and let it rise according to package directions. Roll 2/3 dough into 11" circle on a lightly floured surface. Line bottom and sides of lightly greased 9" cake pan with dough. Place tomatoes and sausage in pan and sprinkle with basil, oregano, salt and pepper. In a separate, medium bowl, mix together Ricotta cheese, spinach, Mozzarella cheese, 3/4 c. Parmesan cheese and garlic. Spread over tomatoes. Roll remaining dough into a 10" circle and place over cheese mixture. Pinch edges to seal. Bake in a preheated 450° oven 25 - 30 minutes. Spread with pizza sauce and sprinkle with remaining 1/4 cup Parmesan cheese. Bake another 10 minutes. Let stand 8 - 10 minutes before slicing.

TUNA NOODLE CASSEROLE
(A classic favorite! The homemade flavor of this dish is unbeatable. It is amazing how such a simplistic, everyday casserole is so well-liked. The creamy texture of this particular recipe is outstanding.)

1 (6 oz.) can tuna, well drained	1 c. sliced mushrooms, partially cooked in butter (optional)
2 c. wide egg noodles, cooked and drained	1 Tbsp. onions, minced
2 c. white sauce*	4 Tbsp. butter
	1 c. plain bread crumbs

Preheat oven to 350°. Lightly butter a 1 1/2 quart baking dish. In a large bowl, combine the tuna, noodles, sauce, mushrooms and onions and carefully mix. Pour into prepared dish. In a medium frying pan, over medium heat, melt butter. Add bread crumbs and toss until they are coated and lightly browned. Sprinkle evenly over the tuna mixture. Cover and bake 25 - 30 minutes, until hot. Let stand 5 - 7 minutes before serving.

*WHITE SAUCE
(This sauce is necessary for use in homemade, creamy dishes. The best way to attain a perfectly smooth sauce is to have the milk hot when added to the butter and flour.)

2 Tbsp. butter	1/2 tsp. salt
2 Tbsp. flour	1/4 tsp. pepper
1 c. milk, heated	

In a heavy-bottomed saucepan, over medium heat, add butter and melt. Stir in the flour and cook, stirring continuously, until the paste cooks and bubbles a little, but do not let it brown, about 2 minutes. Add the hot milk, continuing to stir as the sauce thickens. Bring to a boil. Add salt and pepper, lower the heat and cook, stirring continuously 2 - 3 minutes more. Remove from heat. Use as necessary.

TURKEY DIVAN

(This is an easy, casserole-type dish that tastes delicious and is a great way to use leftover turkey. You may also substitute asparagus spears for broccoli, if desired.)

2 (10 oz.) pkgs. frozen
  broccoli
6 slices turkey breast,
  cooked

6 slices American cheese
1 can cream-of-chicken soup
1 (3 1/2 oz.) can French fried
  onion rings (optional)

Preheat oven to 350°. Cook broccoli according to package directions, until just barely tender. Place broccoli in the bottom of a 9" x 13" baking dish. Cover with turkey slices. Top with cheese slices. Spread soup over cheese. Cover and bake 25 minutes. Remove from oven and sprinkle onion rings on top. Bake another 5 minutes. Let stand 5 - 7 minutes before serving.

TURKEY NOODLE CASSEROLE

(This is another good way to use leftover turkey. This makes a delicious meal in itself as everything you need is already in here. Add freshly baked Biscuits and you're all set!)

3 Tbsp. butter
3 Tbsp. flour
2 1/2 c. milk, heated
1 tsp. parsley
1/2 tsp. salt
1/4 tsp. pepper
2 1/2 c. turkey, cooked
  and coarsely chopped

1/2 c. Parmesan cheese, plus
  1/4 c. (to sprinkle on top)
1 (10 oz.) pkg. frozen broccoli,
  thawed and drained
1 c. wide egg noodles, cooked
  and drained

Preheat oven to 350°. Lightly butter a 2 quart casserole. In a large pan, over medium heat, add butter and melt. Stir in flour and cook, stirring continuously, until paste cooks and bubbles a little, but do not let it brown, about 2 minutes. Add the hot milk, continuing to stir as the sauce thickens. Bring to a boil. Add parsley, salt and pepper. Lower the heat and continue to cook, stirring continuously,

2 - 3 minutes more. Remove from heat. Stir in turkey, 1/2 cup Parmesan cheese and broccoli. Add noodles and gently toss. Pour into prepared casserole. Cover and bake 30 minutes. Remove from oven and sprinkle remaining 1/4 cup Parmesan cheese over top. Bake 10 minutes more. Let stand 5 - 7 minutes before serving.

ZITI

(This is an easy-to-make casserole that everyone loves. It requires little preparation and can be made on a moment's notice as there are very few ingredients and you probably already have them in the kitchen. Of course, you may add your own touch using whatever you like such as fried sausage or Ricotta cheese. This is another dish that is great to bring for a pot-luck dinner, for someone who may be housebound or for a new mother as it can be made ahead of time and refrigerated until ready to bake. This particular recipe is great for a larger crowd but can be easily halved for just four or six.)

1 pound lean ground beef	4 c. tomato sauce
1 large green pepper, chopped	1 pound ziti, cooked and and drained
2 cloves garlic, minced	1 (12 oz.) pkg. Mozzarella cheese, shredded
	1/2 c. Parmesan cheese

Preheat oven to 350°. In a large pan, over medium heat, add ground beef, peppers and garlic. Cook until beef has browned. Drain, if necessary. Add sauce to ground beef mixture and cook 5 - 7 minutes, stirring occasionally. In a 4 quart casserole, pour about 1/2 cup sauce. Top with about 1/3 ziti, 1/3 Mozzarella cheese and 1/3 Parmesan cheese. Repeat layers ending with sauce on top and sprinkling with Parmesan cheese. Cover and bake 35 - 45 minutes. Let stand 5 - 7 minutes before serving.

ZUCCHINI HAMBURGER CASSEROLE

(This casserole is full-of-flavor and is another great way to use the ever popular, delicious zucchini. This is another great dish that travels well and is great for a larger crowd or pot-luck dinner. Of course, you may easily cut this recipe in half, if desired.)

1 - 1 1/2 pounds lean
 ground beef
2 c. white rice, cooked
2 cans cream-of-mushroom
 soup
1 1/2 c. Cheddar cheese,
 shredded

1 tsp. parsley
1/2 tsp. salt
1/4 tsp. pepper
2 medium zucchini, sliced to
 1/4" thickness, par-boiled
1 (10 oz.) container cottage
 cheese, small curd

Preheat oven to 350°. Lightly butter a 3 quart casserole. In a large pan, over medium heat, add ground beef. Cook until browned. Drain, if necessary. Add rice, soup, Cheddar cheese, parsley, salt and pepper. Heat thoroughly, stirring occasionally, about 5 minutes. Remove from heat. Spread about 1/3 ground beef mixture in bottom of prepared casserole. Layer about 1/3 zucchini slices and spread about 1/3 cottage cheese over slices. Repeat layers, ending with cottage cheese on top. Sprinkle extra parsley on top, if desired. Cover and bake 45 minutes. Let stand 5 - 7 minutes before serving.

THE HARRIED HOUSEWIFE SAYS....

If you see me in a harried way,

you'd best be safe and run away!

For chances are, it's plain to see,

my kids are driving me up a tree!

BREADS, ROLLS, MUFFINS

BREADS, ROLLS, MUFFINS

APPLE BREAD

(The addition of walnuts in this delicious bread yields a slightly coarse texture, making this a perfect bread for an afternoon tea or a Sunday brunch. Of course, you may also enjoy it for dessert anytime with a nice cup of Irish Coffee!)

3 Tbsp. milk
2 eggs, lightly beaten
1/2 c. shortening
2 c. flour
1 tsp. baking soda
1 c. sugar

1 c. apples, unpeeled and
  coarsely chopped
1 tsp. cinnamon
1/2 tsp. nutmeg
1/4 tsp. salt
1/2 c. walnuts, chopped

Preheat oven to 350°. Lightly grease a loaf pan. In a large bowl, add all ingredients except walnuts and mix well. (A wooden spoon usually works best.) Mixture will be thick. Stir in nuts. Pour into prepared loaf pan and bake 50 - 55 minutes. Cool in pan 10 minutes before removing to a wire rack. Cool completely before slicing.

Tip: *Whenever using the oven at 350°, always try to have other dishes prepared to go in at the same time. Even if you double up on one recipe, such as making two loaves of bread instead of one, you will save on utility costs in the long run and will be utilizing all available oven space. It seems foolish to turn the oven on for one hour for only one dish, bread or whatever. I always try to make at least two loaves of bread to go into the oven at approximately the same time. You then can freeze one loaf and enjoy one for dessert that night with dinner. There is nothing better than being able to take out a frozen loaf of homemade bread from the freezer when company unexpectedly drops by, microwaving it for a few minutes and enjoying it with a fresh pot of coffee! They will be truly impressed!*

BREADS, ROLLS, MUFFINS

APPLESAUCE BREAD

(This is a moist, delicious bread with just the right amount of spices and nuts. It is not as coarse as Apple Bread but has its own delicate flavor. Of course, it would be great to use homemade applesauce in this recipe but if that's not possible, store-bought applesauce works just as good!)

1/2 c. butter, softened	1 tsp. baking soda
1 c. sugar	1 tsp. cinnamon
1 1/4 c. applesauce	1/2 tsp. nutmeg
1 egg, lightly beaten	1/4 tsp. salt
1 1/2 c. flour	1/2 c. walnuts, chopped

Preheat oven to 350°. Lightly grease a loaf pan. In a large bowl, mix together butter and sugar. Add all other ingredients except walnuts and mix well. Stir in nuts. Pour into prepared loaf pan and bake 55 - 60 minutes. Cool in pan 10 minutes before removing to a wire rack. Serve warm or cooled, as desired.

BANANA BREAD

(This delicious, dark, moist bread is another favorite. The secret to delicious, moist banana bread is using overripe bananas. The smell of this bread baking will surely call them in from outdoors. Enjoy!)

3 overripe bananas, mashed	3/4 c. sugar
2 eggs, lightly beaten	1/2 tsp. salt
2 c. flour	1 tsp. baking soda
	1/2 c. walnuts, chopped

Preheat oven to 350°. Lightly grease a loaf pan. In a large bowl, mix together bananas and eggs. Add all other ingredients except walnuts and mix well. Stir in nuts. Pour into prepared loaf pan and bake 55 - 60 minutes. Cool in pan 10 minutes before removing to a wire rack. Serve warm or cooled, as desired.

BISCUITS

(These biscuits are easy enough to make in a hurry and the taste is undeniably homemade. Nothing smells better baking than biscuits or bread and there's something to be said for fresh-from-the oven biscuits or bread! They just seem to round out a meal! For sweet biscuits, as in making shortcake, add three tablespoons sugar.)

1 1/2 c. flour	1/4 tsp. salt
3 tsp. baking powder	3 Tbsp. shortening
1/2 tsp. baking soda	3/4 c. sour milk*

Preheat oven to 375°. Lightly grease a cookie sheet. In a large bowl, mix together flour, baking powder, baking soda and salt. Add shortening and mix well. Add sour milk and mix well. Drop by tablespoonfuls onto prepared cookie sheet. Bake 8 - 10 minutes, until golden. Cool 1 - 2 minutes on cookie sheet before removing to serving plate.

*SOUR MILK

(This is the easiest way to "sour" milk!)

1 c. milk
1 Tbsp. white vinegar
 or lemon juice

Add 1 tablespoon white vinegar or 1 tablespoon lemon juice to 1 cup of milk and let stand at room temperature 10 - 15 minutes.

BREADS, ROLLS, MUFFINS

BLUEBERRY MUFFINS

(These are the best blueberry muffins you will ever have! They are filled with plenty of blueberries and remind me of old-fashioned, home-baked muffins our grandparents and great-grandparents used to make. I remember picking berries for my grandmother, hoping I would "pick enough" for her to be able to make "something" from the scant amount I came in with. There usually wasn't enough to make a pie but she always managed to make something. This reminds me of those days.)

2 c. flour
2 tsp. baking powder
1/2 tsp. salt
2 1/2 c. blueberries,
  stems removed,
  washed and gently
  patted dry

1/2 c. butter, softened
1 c. sugar plus 2 Tbsp. sugar
  (to sprinkle on top of muffins)
2 eggs
1/2 c. milk
1 tsp. vanilla

Preheat oven to 375°. Line 18 muffin pan cups with paper liners. In a medium bowl, mix together flour, baking powder and salt. In a separate, medium bowl, toss 2 tablespoons of flour mixture with berries. In a large, mixing bowl, beat together butter and 1 cup sugar until light and fluffy. Beat in eggs one at a time. Add remaining flour mixture alternately with milk and vanilla. Remove 1/2 cup berries from bowl and mash. Stir into batter. Fold in remaining berries. Spoon into muffin cups and sprinkle with remaining 2 tablespoons sugar. Bake 25 - 30 minutes. Cool on wire racks.

-73-

BRAN MUFFINS

(These tasty muffins are just what we need on those busy mornings as we head out the door. They also taste great with that first cup of morning coffee. Of course, you may also add raisins, if desired.)

1 egg, lightly beaten	3 tsp. baking powder
1 c. milk	1/4 c. plus 2 tsp. sugar
2 Tbsp. butter, melted	(to sprinkle on top of muffins)
1 c. bran	1/2 tsp. salt
1 c. flour	

Preheat oven to 375°. Line 12 muffin pan cups with paper liners. In a large bowl, mix together egg, milk, butter and bran. Let stand 10 minutes. Add the flour, baking powder, 1/4 cup sugar and salt. Stir gently, just enough to mix. Spoon into muffin cups and sprinkle with remaining sugar. Bake 20 - 25 minutes. Cool on wire racks.

THE HARRIED HOUSEWIFE SAYS....
With all the latest technological advancements in the workplace, is it any wonder we have a better chance of speaking with the President of the United States than to a "real-live" person from the phone company!

BROCCOLI ROLL

(This delicious roll is a lot easier to make than you may think! It makes a great appetizer as well as being a tasty bread to pass around the dinner table. It also is an excellent choice to bring to a friend's house for a party or dinner as just about everyone likes it. Whichever way you choose, you will surely get many compliments.)

2 Tbsp. olive oil
1 (10 oz.) pkg. frozen, chopped broccoli, thawed and drained
2 cloves garlic, minced
1 tsp. oregano
1/2 tsp. salt
1/4 tsp. pepper

1 (1 pound) bag pizza dough (allowed to rise in bag at room temperature)
2 eggs, lightly beaten
1 1/2 c. Mozzarella cheese, shredded
1/4 c. Parmesan cheese

Preheat oven to 350°. In a medium frying pan, on medium heat, add olive oil, broccoli, garlic, oregano, salt and pepper. Cook until broccoli is just tender, about 4 - 5 minutes. On a floured surface, roll out the dough to about 12" x 16" size. Brush half the eggs on the dough. Spread broccoli mixture on dough, to about 1/2" away from edges. Sprinkle Mozzarella cheese and Parmesan cheese on top of broccoli. Roll, jelly-roll style, starting with the long side and tucking edges under as you go. Brush top with remaining eggs. Make three, 1" slits in top of dough. Place on a cookie sheet and bake in oven 30 - 35 minutes or until golden brown. Cool before slicing. Serve warm or cold.

CORN BREAD

(This is an old family favorite. Again, just mixing together a few ingredients you already have can turn an ordinary dinner into a "homey" meal. This delicious texture will remind them of days-gone-by and emphasizes the fact that this delightful, old-fashioned bread never goes out-of-style.)

3/4 c. cornmeal	1/2 tsp. salt
1 c. flour	1 c. milk
1/3 c. sugar	1 egg, beaten
3 tsp. baking powder	2 Tbsp. butter, melted

Preheat oven to 425°. Grease 8" square baking pan. In a large bowl, mix together cornmeal, flour, sugar, baking powder and salt. Add milk, egg and butter and blend well. Pour into prepared pan and bake 20 - 25 minutes. Cool and cut into squares.

THE HARRIED HOUSWIFE SAYS....
You can bet that the day you have your kids plus everybody else's packed in the car to go to the park is the day the car decides to quit right in the middle of the road!

CRANBERRY ORANGE NUT BREAD

(If you really want to impress them, make this bread. It is out-of-this world! I make this bread every year for Christmas and I cannot tell you how many people ask for the recipe. I make this ahead of time and freeze it. When company stops over, this is just what they need on those cold, winter days. You can enjoy it with a nice, hot cup of Irish Coffee, Hot Cocoa or even with a glass of champagne. Although you usually bake it in a large loaf pan (9 1/4" x 5 1/4"), you may also use four mini loaf pans (5 3/4" x 3"). I usually use the four mini loaf pans when the holiday season comes around as I make these breads ahead of time, freeze and give away as gifts. People always enjoy receiving homemade bread. It doesn't get much better.)

3 c. flour	8 Tbsp. butter, melted
3/4 c. sugar	2 eggs, lightly beaten
1 Tbsp. baking powder	1 c. cranberries, stems
1 tsp. salt	removed, washed and patted
1/2 tsp. baking soda	dry then coarsely chopped
1 c. orange juice	3/4 c. walnuts, chopped

Preheat oven to 350°. Grease a large loaf pan (9 1/4" x 5 1/4") or 4 mini loaf pans (5 3/4" x 3"). In a large bowl, mix together flour, sugar, baking powder, salt and baking soda. In a separate, small bowl, mix together orange juice, butter and eggs. Stir into flour mixture, mixing until just moistened. Stir in cranberries and nuts. Pour mixture into prepared pan(s). Bake in large loaf pan 60 - 65 minutes or mini loaf pans 30 - 35 minutes. Cool in pan(s) 10 minutes before removing to wire rack(s).

Tip: *For a one-of-a kind gift idea, make several different kinds of breads, cookies, muffins or whatever you choose. Wrap each one in different colored plastic wrap. Tie a ribbon around each bread or bundle of cookies and place in a big basket. Add a bottle of wine or champagne, a bag of gourmet coffee or whatever they happen to like. Wrap a pretty piece of cellophane around the whole thing. Tie with a decorative ribbon and add a pretty bow. They will love this personal, unique gift.*

DATE NUT BREAD

(A moist, dark bread filled with just enough dates and nuts to add sweetness and a slightly coarse texture. Delicious!)

3/4 c. dates, chopped	1 tsp. baking soda
1/2 c. sugar	1 3/4 c. flour
4 Tbsp. butter	1/2 tsp. salt
1 egg, beaten	3/4 c. walnuts, chopped

Preheat oven to 350°. Lightly grease a loaf pan. In a medium pan, over high heat, bring 3/4 cup water to a boil. Add dates, sugar and butter. Remove from heat and allow to cool to lukewarm. Stir in the egg, baking soda, flour, salt and nuts and blend well. Pour into prepared loaf pan. Bake 50 - 55 minutes. Cool in pan 10 minutes before removing to a wire rack. Serve slightly warm or completely cooled, as desired.

IRISH SODA BREAD

(This is a simple, easy recipe for an old-fashioned favorite. Enjoy it with a cup of hot tea, Irish Coffee or your favorite hot beverage. This is not sweet and is just right for an afternoon tea, Sunday brunch or a snack anytime. Enjoy!)

2 c. flour	2/3 c. milk
4 tsp. baking powder	1/2 c. raisins
1/2 tsp. salt	1 Tbsp. caraway seeds
1 Tbsp. sugar	(optional)
3 Tbsp. butter	

Preheat oven to 375°. Grease a 9" round cake pan. In a large bowl, mix together flour, baking powder, salt and sugar. Cut in the butter with a pastry blender or two knives, then quickly stir the milk into the dough. Add the raisins and caraway seeds, stirring just enough to distribute evenly. On a lightly-floured surface, knead about 20 times. Put dough in prepared pan and bake 20 - 30 minutes. Cool in pan 5 minutes before removing to a wire rack. When cool, cut into wedges and serve.

BREADS, ROLLS, MUFFINS

OATMEAL MUFFINS
(A delicious, not-too-sweet muffin with a coarse, grainy texture that calls out for a big glass of milk, orange juice or coffee to go with it. A great way to start the day!)

1 egg, lightly beaten
1 c. milk
2 Tbsp. butter,
 melted
1 c. quick cooking
 oats

1 c. flour
3 tsp. baking powder
1/3 c. sugar plus 2 tsp. sugar
 (to sprinkle on top of muffins)
1/2 tsp. salt

Preheat oven to 375°. Line 12 muffin pan cups with paper liners. In a large bowl, mix together egg, milk, butter and oats. Let stand 10 minutes. Add flour, baking powder, 1/3 cup sugar and salt and stir, just enough to mix. Spoon into muffin cups and sprinkle with remaining sugar. Bake 20 - 25 minutes. Cool on wire racks.

ORANGE TEACAKES
(This is another old recipe that has been in the family for many years and tastes just as good now as it did then. These are delicious anytime, with afternoon tea, coffee or in the morning as everyone is bustling about. The gentle orange flavor is a delicious change from the usual muffins we have grown accustomed to.)

1 Tbsp. flour plus
 2 c. flour
1/4 c. brown sugar
1 tsp. cinnamon
2 tsp. baking powder
1/4 tsp. baking soda
1 tsp. salt

1/2 c. sugar
1/4 c. orange peel, grated
2/3 c. orange juice
6 Tbsp. butter plus 1 Tbsp.
 butter, melted
2 eggs, lightly beaten

Preheat oven to 375°. Line 18 muffin pan cups with paper liners. In a small bowl, mix together 1 tablespoon flour with brown sugar and cinnamon and set aside. In a medium bowl, mix together 2 cups flour, baking powder, baking soda, salt, sugar and orange peel. Stir in juice, 6 tablespoons butter and eggs. Spoon into muffin cups. Add the 1 tablespoon butter to brown sugar mixture and sprinkle on top of each muffin. Bake 20 - 25 minutes. Cool on wire racks.

PINEAPPLE ZUCCHINI BREAD

(This is a delicious, moist bread that is full-of-flavor. The combination of brown sugar, zucchini and pineapple make this unique bread another frequently requested recipe.)

1 c. firmly packed
  brown sugar
6 Tbsp. butter,
  softened
1 c. zucchini, grated
  (excess juice drained)
1 (8 oz.) can crushed
  pineapple, undrained,
  minus 1 Tbsp. juice

2 eggs, lightly beaten
2 c. flour
1 tsp. baking soda
1 tsp. cinnamon
1/4 tsp. salt
1/2 c. walnuts, chopped

Preheat oven to 350°. Grease 2 loaf pans. In a large mixing bowl, cream together brown sugar and butter until fluffy. Add all other ingredients, except nuts and blend well. Stir in nuts. Pour into prepared pans. Bake 50 - 60 minutes. Cool in pans 10 minutes before removing to wire racks. Cool completely before slicing.

PUMPKIN BREAD

(This is probably the most requested bread recipe of all. The delicious, moist texture blended with just the right amount of cinnamon and just a touch of chocolate make this a bread they will ask for again and again. The best part is, it is so easy to make, you will be able to indulge them often!)

1 1/2 c. flour	2 eggs, beaten
1/2 tsp. salt	1/2 tsp. cinnamon
1 c. sugar	1/4 c. semi-sweet chocolate
1 tsp. baking soda	morsels
1 1/4 c. pumkin	1/4 c. walnuts, chopped
(solid pack, canned)	(optional)
1/4 c. vegetable oil	

Preheat oven to 350°. Grease a loaf pan. In a large bowl, mix together flour, salt, sugar and baking soda. In a separate, medium bowl, mix together pumpkin, oil, eggs, 1/4 cup water and cinnamon. Combine with the dry ingredients but do not mix too thoroughly. Stir in chocolate morsels and nuts. Pour into prepared loaf pan. Bake 50 - 60 minutes. Cool in pan 10 minutes before removing to a wire rack. Cool almost completely before slicing.

RAISIN MUFFINS

(These are easy-to-make, delicious, homemade muffins. Again, the best part is you only use one bowl! This is the best way to bake!)

2 c. flour	1 egg, lightly beaten
3 tsp. baking powder	1 c. milk
1/2 tsp. salt	4 Tbsp. butter, melted
2 Tbsp. sugar plus	1/3 c. raisins
2 tsp. (to sprinkle on	
top of muffins)	

Preheat oven to 375°. Line 12 muffin pan cups with paper liners. In a large bowl, mix together flour, baking powder, salt and 2 tablespoons sugar. Add the egg, milk and butter, stirring only enough to mix. Gently stir in raisins. Spoon into muffin cups. Sprinkle with remaining 2 teaspoons sugar. Bake 20 - 25 minutes. Cool on wire racks.

SAUSAGE ROLL
(This is always a favorite. It is so easy-to-make and so many people enjoy it, you will find them asking you to make it again and again.)

1 pound loose, Italian sausage, hot, medium or mild	2 eggs, lightly beaten
1 tsp. oregano	1 1/2 c. Mozzarella cheese, shredded
1 (1 pound) bag pizza dough (allowed to rise in bag at room temperature)	1/4 c. Parmesan cheese

Preheat oven to 350°. In a medium frying pan, on medium heat, add sausage and oregano. Cook until sausage is no longer pink. Drain. On a floured surface, roll out dough to about 12" x 16" size. Brush half the eggs on the dough. Spread sausage on dough, to about 1/2" away from edges. Sprinkle Mozzarella cheese and Parmesan cheese on top of sausage. Roll, jelly-roll style, starting with the long side and tucking edges under as you go. Brush top with remaining eggs. Make three, 1" slits in top of dough. Place on a cookie sheet and bake in oven 30 - 35 minutes or until golden brown. Cool before slicing. Serve warm or cold.

SPINACH ROLL

(Another delicious, easy-to-make roll. This travels well and can be used for so many different things. A good idea for a large gathering is to make Broccoli, Sausage and Spinach Rolls ahead of time, slice and place them on a large platter. Serve along with pizza and tossed salad and you will have a delicious assortment of homemade goodies! Be prepared though, the Rolls will not last long!)

2 Tbsp. olive oil
1 (10 oz.) pkg. frozen,
  chopped spinach,
  thawed and drained
2 cloves garlic, minced
1 tsp. oregano
1/2 tsp. salt
1/4 tsp. pepper

1 (1 pound) bag pizza dough
  (allowed to rise in bag at room
  temperature)
2 eggs, lightly beaten
1 1/2 c. Mozzarella cheese,
  shredded
1/4 c. Parmesan cheese

Preheat oven to 350°. In a medium frying pan, on medium heat, add olive oil, spinach, garlic, oregano, salt and pepper. Cook until spinach is just tender, about 4 - 5 minutes. On a floured surface, roll out the dough to about 12" x 16" size. Brush half the eggs on the dough. Spread spinach mixture on dough, to about 1/2" away from edges. Sprinkle Mozzarella cheese and Parmesan cheese on top of spinach. Roll, jelly-roll style, starting with the long side and tucking edges under as you go. Brush top with remaining eggs. Make three, 1" slits in top of dough. Place on a cookie sheet and bake in oven 30 - 35 minutes or until golden brown. Cool before slicing. Serve warm or cold.

STRAWBERRY BREAD

(This is a delicious, moist bread that is full-of-flavor. This is great to have in the morning as you are hurrying out the door or to pass around the dinner table. It also makes a tasty dessert. Although this recipe calls for one cup fresh strawberries, in a pinch you may use one cup strawberry preserves. This recipe makes two loaves and believe me, you will need these two loaves as this unique, delicately-flavored bread will not last long.)

8 Tbsp. butter, softened
1 1/2 c. sugar
1 tsp. vanilla
1 tsp. salt
1 tsp. lemon juice
4 eggs
1/2 tsp. baking soda

1/2 c. sour cream
3 c. flour
1/2 c. walnuts, chopped
1 c. fresh strawberries, washed, hulled and mashed
1 Tbsp. red food color (optional)

Preheat oven to 350°. Grease 2 loaf pans. In a large mixing bowl, add butter, sugar, vanilla, salt and lemon juice. Beat well. Add eggs and beat well. In a small bowl, add baking soda and sour cream and mix well. Stir into butter and egg mixture. Fold in flour, nuts, strawberries and food color. Pour into prepared loaf pans. Bake 35 - 45 minutes. Cool in pans 10 minutes before removing to wire racks. Cool completely before slicing.

THE HARRIED HOUSEWIFE SAYS....
It never ceases to amaze me how some people offer so much "free" advice but never seem to follow their own!

WHOLE WHEAT BREAD

(This is a tasty addition to any table. The consistency of this bread is slightly coarse, heavy, dark and moist. It definitely has that authentic "homemade" appeal. They will think you spent hours making it. They do not have to know the truth! Enjoy!)

1/2 c. white flour
1 tsp. baking powder
1 tsp. baking soda
1 tsp. salt
2 c. whole-wheat flour

4 Tbsp. butter, melted
1 1/2 c. buttermilk (or 1 1/2 c.
  plain yogurt)
1/2 c. molasses

Preheat oven to 375°. Grease a loaf pan. In a large bowl, mix together the white flour, baking powder, baking soda, salt and whole-wheat flour. Add butter, buttermilk and molasses and stir until blended. Pour into prepared pan and bake 50 - 60 minutes. Cool in pan 10 minutes before removing to a wire rack. Serve warm or cooled, as desired.

Tip: When a recipe calls for buttermilk, you may substitute plain yogurt in equal amounts without sacrificing the flavor.

ZUCCHINI BREAD

(This recipe has been around for years and is still my personal favorite! I have tried many other zucchini breads but still prefer this one. If you are looking for a simple, delicious, heavy and moist zucchini bread, this is the one for you. There is just enough cinnamon and vanilla to add a light, delicate flavor without being overpowering. This recipe emphasizes the fact that simple, old-fashioned flavor never goes out-of-style.)

2 1/4 c. sugar	**3 eggs, lightly beaten**
8 Tbsp. butter, softened	**2 1/2 c. flour**
1/2 c. shortening	**2 tsp. vanilla**
2 c. zucchini, peeled,	**1 tsp. baking powder**
grated and drained	**1 tsp. cinnamon**
of any excess juice	**1/2 tsp. salt**

Preheat oven to 350°. Grease 2 loaf pans. In a large mixing bowl, cream together sugar, butter and shortening until fluffy. Add all other ingredients and blend well. Pour into prepared loaf pans and bake 55 - 60 minutes. Cool in pans 10 minutes before removing to wire racks. Cool completely before slicing.

Tip: Whenever grating zucchini for a particular bread recipe, you may notice there is a lot of "juice" from it. In most cases, you do not need this juice and adding it may cause the bread to become extremely moist and "chewy." You do not want this to happen! Always drain the grated zucchini in a colander and with the back of a big, wooden spoon, gently press the zucchini against the side of the colander to squeeze out most of the excess moisture. Believe me, I did not always know to do this which unfortunately, resulted in many ultra chewy zucchini breads!

DESSERTS

DESSERTS

APPLE CAKE

(This is a coarse, moist, delicious cake with just the right amount of cinnamon and chopped walnuts. It is probably one of the easiest cakes to make as well. When mixing it, you will notice that the batter is very thick. This is how it is supposed to be. You may also think there is not enough to fill a 9" x 13" pan but spread it evenly into prepared pan and it will rise sufficiently. You may frost with Cream Cheese Frosting, if desired. You will be happily surprised at how good this cake is. It happens to be my husband's favorite. Enjoy!)

2 c. flour
1 3/4 c. sugar
3/4 c. vegetable oil
2 eggs, lightly beaten
3/4 tsp. baking soda
1/2 tsp. salt

1 tsp. cinnamon
1/2 tsp. nutmeg
1 Tbsp. vanilla
4 1/4 c. apples, peeled and
   diced
1 c. walnuts, chopped

Preheat oven to 350°. Lightly grease and flour a 9" x 13" baking pan. In a large bowl, mix together all ingredients except apples and nuts. Gently stir in apples and nuts. Pour into prepared pan. Bake 45 minutes. Cool completely before frosting.

Tip. When buying apples, keep in mind that green apples such as Granny Smiths are tart, keep well and are good for a snack. However, when used for baking, Red Delicious and Cortland, if available, are your best bet.

DESSERTS

APPLE CRISP

(This is a delicious dessert to make for company. You can put it into the oven just as you sit down for dinner and it should be done just in time to enjoy for dessert. It smells so good baking, they won't be able to wait! You may easily cut this recipe in half if making it just for four or six. Serve warm, with vanilla ice-cream, or freshly whipped cream, if desired.)

10 large, firm apples, peeled and sliced	**1/2 tsp. salt**
2 c. flour	**2 eggs, lightly beaten**
1 3/4 c. sugar	**3/4 c. butter, melted**
2 tsp. baking powder	**1 tsp. cinnamon**
	1/2 tsp. nutmeg

Preheat oven to 350°. Lightly grease a 9" x 13" baking pan. Pile apples in. In a medium bowl, mix together flour, sugar, baking powder, salt and eggs. Spoon on top of apples and gently spread over all. Pour melted butter over flour mixture and sprinkle with cinnamon and nutmeg. Bake 45 - 50 minutes. Cool slightly before serving.

Tip: To make freshly whipped cream, put beaters in the freezer a few minutes before beating. In a large mixing bowl, add 1/2 pint whipping cream, 1/2 teaspoon sugar and about 1/4 teaspoon vanilla, if desired. Beat on high just until soft peaks form. Be careful that you do not beat too long as cream that is beaten too long will begin to turn to butter.

APPLE PIE

(Nothing tastes better than fresh-from-the oven, homemade apple pie. And certainly nothing smells better while baking. This classic, easy-to-make recipe is sure to be a favorite.)

pastry dough for 9"	**1/2 tsp. nutmeg**
two-crust pie	**1 1/2 Tbsp. flour**
3/4 c. sugar	**6 large, firm apples**
1/2 tsp. salt	**1 tsp. lemon juice**
1 1/2 tsp. cinnamon	**2 Tbsp. butter, cubed**

Preheat oven to 425°. Line a 9" pie pan with half the pastry dough. In a large bowl, mix together sugar, salt, cinnamon, nutmeg and flour. Peel, core and slice the apples and gently stir them into the sugar mixture, being sure to coat them well. Pile them into the lined pan and sprinkle lemon juice over all. Dot with the butter. Drape the top crust over pie. Crimp the edges and cut several vents in the top. Bake 10 minutes, then lower the heat to 350° and bake 30 - 40 minutes more, until the apples are tender and the crust has browned. Cool before slicing.

Tip: *While homemade pastry dough is certainly the preferred choice in baking, you may easily sustitute pre-made, store-bought dough if you simply do not have the time to roll out dough. If it comes down to whether you will bake a pie or not depending on whether you have to roll out dough, grab the pre-made, store-bought dough and fill with your favorite filling. Your friends and family will be just as happy!*

DESSERTS

BLUEBERRY CAKE
(This is about as good as it gets! Fresh blueberries mixed with just the right amount of sugar and vanilla make this a delicious, moist, old-fashioned flavored cake. Just a few of the right ingredients mixed together can make all the difference in the world.)

1 c. butter, softened	1/2 tsp. salt
2 c. sugar	1 tsp. baking powder
4 eggs	1 pt. fresh blueberries, stems
1 tsp. vanilla	removed, washed and gently
3 c. flour	patted dry

Preheat oven to 325°. Grease a tube (Bundt) pan with butter and sprinkle with granulated sugar, about 1/4 cup. In a large mixing bowl, cream together butter and sugar. Add eggs and beat until fluffy. Add vanilla and mix well. In a separate, medium bowl, mix together flour, salt and baking powder. Remove 1 cup flour mixture from bowl and reserve. Add remaining flour to butter, sugar and egg mixture and beat well. In a medium bowl, add reserved flour mixture and blueberries. Gently stir. Fold into batter. Spoon into prepared pan. Bake 1 - 1 1/4 hours. Cool in pan 15 minutes. Invert onto wire rack and completely cool before slicing.

Tip: *When buying blueberries, look for a bright, blue color and a slightly frosted look. They should be firm, dry and well-rounded. Of course if you are lucky enough to live in an area where blueberries grow wild, by all means grab a bucket and pick as many as you can! Consider yourself very lucky to be able to enjoy such a simple pleasure.*

BLUEBERRY COBBLER

(A not-too-sweet dessert that is served warm and calls out for a dollop of freshly whipped cream on top. This is another recipe that is good to make for company as it smells so good baking and if put into the oven at the start of dinner, will have cooled just enough to be ready to serve for dessert at just the right time. You may also use peaches in place of blueberries, if desired, or any other fresh fruit.)

3 1/2 c. fresh blueberries,   1 c. flour
    stems removed, washed   1 c. sugar
    and gently patted dry   1/2 tsp. salt
1 Tbsp. lemon juice   1 egg, beaten
1/4 tsp. almond extract   6 Tbsp. butter, melted

Preheat oven to 375°. Butter a 10" x 6" pan. Place blueberries on bottom. Sprinkle with lemon juice and almond extract. In a medium bowl, mix together flour and sugar. Add egg and mix with a fork (or freshly washed hands!) until crumbly. Sprinkle over blueberries. Drizzle with butter. Bake 35 - 40 minutes. Cool slightly before serving.

Tip: If you happen to have extra blueberries, put them into a bowl, add a little cream and a little sugar and revel in the wondrous taste of nature's bounty!

BLUEBERRY PIE

(Another delicious, old-fashioned, simple pie. Again, just a few ingredients mixed together and there you have it, a work-of-art. There is nothing better than homemade, fresh-from-the oven pie. They will thank you again and again.)

pastry dough for 9"	**1 Tbsp. lemon juice**
two-crust pie	**1 Tbsp. butter, cubed**
3 Tbsp. flour	
3/4 c. sugar	
1/8 tsp. salt	
4 c. (1 qt.) fresh blueberries,	
stems removed, washed and	
gently patted dry	

Preheat oven to 425°. Line the pie pan with half the pastry dough. In a large bowl, mix together the flour, sugar and salt. Add the blueberries and lemon juice and toss well. Pile the mixture into the lined pan and dot with butter. Drap the top crust over pie. Crimp edges and cut several vents in the top. Bake 10 minutes, then lower the heat to 350° and bake 30 - 40 minutes or until top has browned. Cool before slicing.

THE HARRIED HOUSEWIFE SAYS....
The uncanny ability to laugh at oneself in the face of adversity is just about the most charming personality trait one can possess.

BROWNIES

(These are moist, dark and sinfully delicious! This particular recipe calls for melted chocolate. You may melt it on the stove in a heavy saucepan over low heat, stirring continuously, or may even microwave it until just melted. These are sure to be a favorite!)

1 c. butter, softened	4 oz. unsweetened chocolate,
2 c. sugar	melted
1 tsp. vanilla	1 c. flour
4 eggs	1 c. walnuts, chopped

Preheat oven to 350°. Butter a 9" x 13" baking pan. In a large mixing bowl, cream together butter, sugar and vanilla. Add eggs and beat well. Stir in cooled chocolate. Add flour and nuts and gently stir. Pour into prepared pan. Bake 25 - 30 minutes. Cool completely before cutting into squares. Sprinkle confectioners' sugar over top, if desired.

CARAMEL FUDGE CAKE

(This is a lucious, dark cake with a surprise hidden in the middle. After a delicious meal, this will definitely hit the spot. Everyone will like this one.)

1 pkg. Devil's food cake	6 Tbsp. butter
mix	1 (14 oz.) can sweetened
1 (14 oz.) pkg. caramels,	condensed milk
unwrapped	1 c. walnuts, chopped

Preheat oven to 350°. Lightly grease a 9" x 13" baking pan. Prepare cake mix according to package directions. Pour 2 cups batter into prepared pan and bake 15 minutes. In a heavy saucepan, over low heat, melt caramels and butter with sweetened condensed milk, stirring constantly until smooth. Spread evenly over cake. Spread remaining batter over caramel mixture. Top with nuts. Return to oven and bake 30 - 35 minutes more. Cool almost completely before slicing.

DESSERTS

CARROT CAKE
(This is a moist, coarse cake with just the right amount of cinnamon. The chopped walnuts add that extra bit of hearty flavor making this exceptional cake a favorite. For a truly authentic taste, frost with Cream Cheese Frosting and sprinkle extra chopped walnuts over top.)

2 c. flour
2 c. sugar
1 1/2 tsp. baking soda
1/2 tsp. salt
2 tsp. cinnamon

1 1/2 c. vegetable oil
4 eggs
3 c. carrots, peeled and freshly
  grated
1 c. walnuts, chopped

Preheat oven to 350°. Grease and four a 9" x 13" baking pan. In a large mixing bowl, mix together flour, sugar, baking soda, salt and cinnamon. Add oil and eggs and beat well. Stir in carrots and nuts. Pour into prepared pan and bake 45 - 50 minutes. Cool before frosting.

Tip: To keep peeled carrots fresh and crisp until ready to use, place in a bowl and cover with cold water. Add a couple drops of lemon juice. This will also aid in helping carrots retain their bright orange color.

CHEESECAKE

(This is your classic cheesecake recipe. It is easy-to-make and tastes delicious. A cup of hot, fresh coffee would certainly fare well with this delicious, rich and creamy cake. You do not need to use a springform pan for this recipe as a 9" round pie pan works best. Top with strawberries, blueberries, cherries or your favorite fruit. Of course, it tastes delicious plain.)

2 (8 oz.) pkgs. cream cheese, softened	2 eggs 3/4 c. graham cracker crumbs
1/2 c. sugar	1 1/4 c. strawberies, sliced
3/4 tsp. vanilla	(or your favorite fruit)

Preheat oven to 350°. In a 9" pie pan, spray bottom and sides with no-stick cooking spray. In a large mixing bowl, mix together cream cheese, sugar and vanilla. Add eggs and mix well. Sprinkle crumbs on bottom of pan and pat gently. Pour cream cheese mixture into prepared pie pan. Bake 40 - 45 minutes or until center is almost set. Refrigerate at least 3 hours or overnight. Top with strawberries or your favorite fruit.

Tip: When making cheesecake, the longer you allow it chill, at least three hours but preferrably eight hours or even overnight, the better it will taste.

CHEESECAKE CHOCOLATE AMARETTO

(This cake tastes so good and looks so enticing garnished with Chocolate Curls, they will wonder if you bought it at a gourmet bakery! Such a rich, deliciously decadent dessert will have them asking for a second and quite possibly, third piece! Go ahead and indulge their cravings. This cake is so good, you can't blame them! And while you're at it, why not cut yourself an extra slice too. After all, you deserve it!)

8 chocolate wafers, finely crushed	1/2 c. flour
2 (8 oz.) pkgs. cream cheese, softened	1/2 c. Amaretto
1 1/4 c. sugar	1 1/2 tsp. vanilla
1 c. cottage cheese, small curd	1/4 tsp. salt
1/2 c. cocoa	2 eggs
	1/4 c. semi-sweet chocolate morsels
	chocolate curls*

Preheat oven to 300°. Lightly spray bottom and side of 8" springform pan with no-stick cooking spray. Sprinkle chocolate wafer crumbs in bottom of prepared pan. Set aside. In a large mixing bowl, mix together cream cheese, sugar, cottage cheese, cocoa, flour, Amaretto, vanilla and salt until smooth. Add eggs and beat until blended. Fold in chocolate morsels. Slowly pour mixture over crumbs in pan. Bake 45 - 50 minutes or until center is almost set. Cool in pan. Chill at least 8 hours or overnight. Remove sides of pan and transfer cheesecake to a serving platter. Garnish with chocolate curls.

*CHOCOLATE CURLS
(These add visual appeal and taste great.)

3 squares semi-sweet chocolate

In a heavy saucepan, over low heat, add chocolate and stir continuously until melted (or microwave until just melted). Pour melted chocolate onto wax paper and spread to a 3" wide strip. Let stand until cool but not firm. Pull a vegetable peeler across the chocolate and transfer to a plate. Refrigerate until ready-to-use.

CHEESECAKE SQUARES
(These delicious, creamy squares are great for a party or any occasion. They travel well and everyone loves them. Be sure to refrigerate at least three hours before cutting into squares. Top with your favorite fruit, if desired.)

3/4 c. graham cracker crumbs
3/4 c. sugar, separated
3 Tbsp. butter, melted
1 (16 oz.) container cottage cheese, small curd

1 (8 oz.) pkg. cream cheese, softened
3 eggs
1 c. sour cream
1 tsp. vanilla

Preheat oven to 350°. In a medium bowl, mix together crumbs, 1 tablespoon sugar and butter. Sprinkle into bottom of 9" x 13" baking pan and pat gently. Bake 10 minutes. Remove from oven. Reduce heat to 300°. In a large mixing bowl, mix together cottage cheese, cream cheese and 1/2 cup sugar. Add eggs and beat until well blended. Pour over slightly cooled crust. Bake 45 minutes. In a medium bowl, mix together sour cream, remaining sugar and vanilla. Spread evenly over cheesecake. Bake 10 minutes more. Cool completely. Refrigerate until ready to serve. When ready to serve, cut into squares. Garnish with your favorite fruit, if desired.

Tip: While using fresh fruit to top cake, particularly cheesecake, is the preferred method, you may easily substitute canned fruit for fresh fruit without sacrificing the flavor.

CHOCOLATE CAKE

(This is a deep, dark chocolate cake that is deliciously moist. If you are a chocolate lover, as I am, this is the cake for you! After trying it, you will definitely find yourself making it again and again. This particular recipe calls for two cups cold coffee which adds to the rich flavor. However, you will not taste the coffee. You will notice the mixture is thin but this is how it's supposed to be. I usually frost with Frosting, Whipped Cream using chocolate pudding. It doesn't get much easier than this and the compliments you will receive will make your day! Enjoy!)

2 c. flour	2 eggs
2 c. sugar	1 c. vegetable oil
1 c. cocoa	2 tsp. vanilla
2 tsp. baking soda	2 cups cold coffee
1 1/2 tsp. salt	

Preheat oven to 350°. Grease and lightly flour a 9" x 13" baking pan. In a large bowl, mix together flour, sugar, cocoa, baking soda and salt. Add eggs, vegetable oil, vanilla and coffee. Mix well. Pour into prepared pan. Bake 45 - 50 minutes. Cool completely before frosting.

THE HARRIED HOUSEWIFE SAYS....
*Warning! If you are in my living room and you happen to drop some change onto the floor and it rolls under the couch, you will be entering your hand under the couch **at your own risk** as it is possible, even probable, that you will not only be able to retrieve your change but may also discover a few other items (living or otherwise). A list of these might include (but are not limited to) a doll or certain appendage of doll, crayon or piece of crayon, popcorn, tissue, book or gamepiece. Good luck in your retrieval!*

CHOCOLATE CHESS PIE

(This is a great pie to make if you don't have a lot of time and want something homemade and delicious. Just mix everything together, you probably already have everything in your kitchen, and pour into lined pie pan. No need for too much forethought or preparation! Add a little bit of freshly whipped cream on each slice of cooled pie, if desired.)

pastry dough for 9"	1 (5 oz.) can evaporated milk
one-crust pie	8 Tbsp. butter, melted and
1 1/4 c. sugar	cooled
2 Tbsp. flour	2 eggs, lightly beaten
3 Tbsp. cocoa	1 1/2 tsp. vanilla

Preheat oven to 350°. Line pie pan with pastry dough. In a large bowl, mix together sugar, flour and cocoa. Add all other ingredients and mix well. Pour into prepared pan. Bake 40 - 45 minutes. Cool completely before serving.

CHOCOLATE CHIP CAKE

(Another easy, delicious cake that can be made quickly and tastes as if you spent hours on it. They will never know! Frost with Frosting, Cocoa, if desired.)

1 pkg. chocolate cake mix	3 eggs
1 (3.4) box instant	1 1/4 c. water
chocolate pudding	1 c. chocolate chips

Preheat oven to 350°. Lightly grease and flour a 9" x 13" baking pan. In a large bowl, mix together cake mix and pudding. Add eggs and mix well. Stir in water and mix well. Add chocolate chips and stir gently. Pour into prepared pan and bake 40 - 45 minutes. Cool completely before frosting.

DESSERTS

CHOCOLATE DIPPED STRAWBERRIES
*(Such a delicious treat! Add a bottle of chilled champagne and
have a romantic rendezvous!)*

2 pts. large strawberries　　**8 (1 oz.) squares semi-sweet**
(about 28), at room　　　　　**chocolate**
temperature

At least one hour before serving, rinse strawberries with running
cold water but do not remove stems. With paper towels, pat
completely dry. Line a cookie sheet with wax paper. In a small,
heavy saucepan, over low heat, add chocolate and cook, stirring
continuously, until melted and smooth. Remove from heat. Hold
strawberries, one at a time, and dip into melted chocolate, leaving
part of strawberry uncovered. Shake off excess chocolate and place
on lined cookie sheet. Refrigerate until ready to serve.

*Tip: When buying strawberries, look for bright, red, shiny berries
which are well-formed. If there are stains on the container, do not
buy them as this may indicate spoilage. A good way to enjoy fresh
strawberries is with heavy cream, whipped cream or yogurt. Of
course, they also taste great added to cereals.*

CHOCOLATE NUT PUDDING DELIGHT
(If you really want to impress them, make this dessert! It is sinfully delicious with its rich, creamy texture and crust made with chopped nuts. A melt-in-your mouth pleasure, this dessert is to die for! Enjoy!)

6 Tbsp. butter, melted
1 3/4 c. flour
1/2 c. walnuts, chopped
1 pt. whipping cream
1 (8 oz.) pkg. cream cheese,
  softened

1 c. confectioners' sugar
2 (3.4 oz.) boxes instant
  chocolate pudding
3 c. milk

Preheat oven to 350°. In a large bowl, mix together butter, flour and nuts. Press into bottom of 9" x 13" baking pan. Bake 15 minutes. Remove from oven and cool. In a large mixing bowl, add whipping cream and beat until peaks form. Take out 1 cup whipped cream and set aside. Add softened cream cheese and confectioners' sugar to remaining whipped cream and mix well. Spread on cooled crust. In a separate, large bowl, add pudding with milk and mix until thickened. Spread on cheese mixture. Spread reserved whipped cream on top. Sprinkle with chopped nuts, if desired. Refrigerate until ready to serve.

THE HARRIED HOUSEWIFE SAYS....
The key to a happy marriage isn't communication. It's marrying someone who will cook and clean when you don't feel like it!

CHOCOLATE PECAN BARS

(This is another dessert everyone likes. They don't take long to make and taste so good, they won't last long either! You may substitute chopped walnuts or your favorite nuts in place of pecans, if desired.)

1 c. light brown sugar,	2 c. flour
firmly packed	1/4 tsp. salt
1 c. butter, softened	1 3/4 c. semi-sweet chocolate
1 egg	morsels
1 tsp. vanilla	1/2 c. pecans, chopped

Preheat oven to 350°. Grease a 9" x 13" baking pan. In a large mixing bowl, mix together brown sugar, butter, egg and vanilla. Blend in flour and salt. Press mixture into prepared pan. Bake 25 - 30 minutes or until lightly browned. Remove from oven and immediately sprinkle chocolate morsels on crust. Let stand until softened, about 5 minutes. Spread evenly over crust. Sprinkle with pecans. Cool completely. Cut into bars.

Tip: To store chocolate, whether unsweetened, semi-sweet or sweet, keep it wrapped and in a cool place but not in the refrigerator. When chocolate is exposed to air over a long period of time, it sometimes becomes discolored and crumbly. However, this does not mean that it is stale and is still perfectly usable.

CHRISTMAS OR CUT OUT COOKIES

(These are Colleen's and Kelly's favorite cookies to make and favorite cookies to eat. Of course, these are great for the holidays but you may make these any time of the year as children, in particular, delight in making them so much. Of course they have just as much fun decorating them as they do making them.)

1 c. butter, softened	2 tsp. baking powder
1 c. sugar	1 tsp. vanilla
1 egg	2 3/4 c. flour

Preheat oven to 400°. In a large mixing bowl, cream together butter and sugar. Add egg and vanilla and mix well. Add baking powder and flour, one cup at a time, mixing after each addition. You may want to use a wooden spoon as dough will become very stiff. Blend last 3/4 cup of flour by hand. Do not chill dough. Divide into 2 balls. On a floured surface, roll each ball into a circle about 12" in diameter and 1/4" thick. Dip cutters in flour before use. Bake cookies on ungreased cookie sheet(s) on top rack of oven 7 - 10 minutes or until cookies are lightly browned. Cool on cookie sheet(s) 2 - 3 minutes before removing to wire racks. Cool completely before frosting, if desired.

THE HARRIED HOUSEWIFE SAYS....
While there is no doubt that baking cookies with a child can be a very harrowing experience, from rolling out the dough to cutting them into their "favorite" shape and finally decorating the finished product, it can also be one of the most rewarding things we can do with a child. The mess that it makes is hardly comparable to the memories that it makes. If you are lucky enough to have a child or children in your life, whether they are yours or someone else's, consider yourself lucky as you are a very rich person. And remember....take care of your precious treasures. After all, they're "all you've got."

DESSERTS

COCONUT CRISPIES
(These chewy cookies go great with afternoon tea, coffee or your favorite beverage. They make delicious snacks as well. Of course, you may easily double this recipe. Whichever way you choose, you are sure to enjoy these tasty little cookies.)

1 egg white	**1/2 tsp. almond extract**
1/2 c. sugar	**1/4 tsp. vanilla**
1/2 c. coconut	**1/8 tsp. salt**
1 c. cornflakes	

Preheat oven to 350°. Lightly grease a cookie sheet. In a large mixing bowl, add egg white and beat until stiff. Add all other ingredients. Drop by teaspoonfuls onto prepared cookie sheet. Bake 8 - 10 minutes or until edges are lightly browned. Cool on cookie sheet 2 - 3 minutes before removing to a wire rack. Serve warm, if desired.

COCONUT MACAROONS
(This is another delightful cookie. The chewy consistency and gentle almond flavor make this a favorite family recipe.)

1 1/2 c. coconut	**1/8 tsp. salt**
1/3 c. sugar	**2 egg whites**
3 Tbsp. flour	**1 tsp. almond extract**

Preheat oven to 325°. Lightly grease cookie sheets. In a medium bowl, mix together coconut, sugar, flour and salt. Add egg whites and almond extract and stir gently. Drop by teaspoonfuls onto prepared cookie sheets. Bake 10 - 12 minutes. Cool 2 - 3 minutes before removing to wire racks. Serve warm, if desired.

COFFEE CAKE

(This recipe has been in the family for many years. While it is moist and delicious, the best part is discovering the Nut Topping hidden in the middle of the cake as well as being sprinkled on top. There is nothing better than an old-fashioned, tried and true recipe!)

6 Tbsp. butter, softened
1 c. sugar
2 eggs
1 tsp. vanilla
2 c. flour

1 tsp. baking powder
1 tsp. baking soda
1/2 tsp. salt
1 c. sour cream
Nut Topping*

*NUT TOPPING

1/4 c. sugar
1 tsp. cinnamon

1/2 c. walnuts, chopped

Preheat oven to 350°. Grease and flour tube (Bundt) pan. In a large mixing bowl, mix together butter, sugar, eggs and vanilla until light and fluffy. Add flour, baking powder, baking soda and salt and mix well. Add sour cream and blend. In a medium bowl, mix together ingredients for Nut Topping. Pour half of cake mixture into prepared pan. Sprinkle half of Nut Topping over then pour remaining cake mixture. Top with remaining Nut Topping. Bake 45 - 55 minutes. Cool in pan 15 minutes. Invert onto wire rack to finish cooling. May serve slightly warm, as desired.

CREAM CHEESE BROWNIES

(These luscious brownies are out-of-this world! Cream cheese swirled in moist, heavenly richness is a chocolate lover's dream come true! After they try these, you will be asked to make them many times over. These are great to make ahead and bring along for a picnic or to a friend's house as they travel well and are sure to be liked by many.)

1/2 c. semi-sweet chocolate morsels	5 eggs
3 oz. unsweetened chocolate	2 tsp. vanilla, divided
3/4 c. butter, softened	1 c. flour
2 c. sugar, divided	1/4 tsp. salt
	2 (8 oz.) pkgs. cream cheese, softened

Preheat oven to 325°. Butter bottom and sides of 9" x 13" baking pan. In a heavy saucepan, over low heat, add semi-sweet chocolate morsels and unsweetened chocolate. Cook, stirring continuously until melted. Remove from heat. Cool slightly. In a medium mixing bowl, mix together butter and 1 cup of sugar. Add 3 eggs and beat well. Stir in melted chocolate and 1 teaspoon vanilla. Mix until smooth. Stir in flour and salt. Take out 1 cup of chocolate mixture and set aside. Spread remaining chocolate mixture in the bottom of prepared pan. In a medium mixing bowl, mix together cream cheese, remaining 1 cup of sugar and remaining 1 teaspoon of vanilla. Beat well. Add remaining eggs, one at a time, beating well after each addition. Spread the cream cheese mixture over the chocolate. Scatter spoonfuls of reserved chocolate over the cream cheese. With a knife, swirl the chocolate into the cream cheese mixture. Bake 50 - 55 minutes. Cool completely. Cut into squares.

CREME DE MENTHE BARS

(If you are looking for something a little different and uniquely impressive, this is the dessert for you. The Creme De Menthe adds just enough flavor making these bars a one-of-a kind delectable treat. This dessert travels well and would be great to bring to a friend's house for dessert or to simply enjoy anytime, especially when we crave something sweet!)

1 c. sugar
1 c. butter, softened, divided
4 eggs, beaten
1 c. flour
1 tsp. vanilla

1 (16 oz.) can chocolate syrup
2 c. confectioners' sugar
2 Tbsp. Creme De Menthe liqueur
topping*

*TOPPING

1 c. semi-sweet chocolate morsels

6 tsp. butter

Preheat oven to 350°. Lightly butter a 9" x 13" baking pan. In a large mixing bowl, mix together sugar, 1/2 cup butter, eggs, flour, vanilla and chocolate syrup. Pour into prepared pan. Bake 30 minutes. Remove from oven and cool. In a large mixing bowl, mix together confectioners' sugar, remaining 1/2 cup butter and Creme De Menthe. Spread on cooled cake. In a heavy saucepan, over low heat, add semi-sweet chocolate morsels and butter and cook, stirring continuously, until melted. Spread on top of Creme De Menthe mixture. Cool. Cut into bars.

DESSERTS

ENGLISH TRIFLE

(Such a delicious treat! This looks so good, and tastes even better. Great with afternoon tea, coffee or your favorite beverage. This is an excellent dessert to make for company as it looks so appealing, especially if served in a trifle bowl. If you do not have a trifle bowl, a clear 12 cup serving bowl works well.)

3 c. light cream	1/2 c. raspberry jam
5 egg yolks	1/2 c. sherry
1/4 c. sugar	1 c. whipping cream
1/4 c. cornstarch	1/2 c. slivered almonds, toasted
2 tsp. vanilla	(optional)
1 sponge cake	
(approximately 10 oz.)	

In a large bowl, whisk together 1/4 cup cream, egg yolks, sugar and cornstarch. In a heavy saucepan, over medium heat, add remaining cream and heat until steaming, stirring constantly. Gradually whisk it into the egg-yolk mixture. Return the mixture to the saucepan and cook over medium heat, whisking until thickened, about 3 - 4 minutes. Remove from heat and stir in vanilla. Pour into a bowl. Press a piece of plastic wrap onto the custard surface to prevent a skin from forming. Refrigerate. Cut cake into 2" thick slices and cut slices into 1" x 4" strips. Spread jam over one side of each strip. Arrange half the cake, jam side up, in the bottom of a 12 cup serving bowl. Drizzle with half the sherry. In a medium mixing bowl, beat whipping cream until peaks form. Fold cream into custard mixture. Spoon half the custard mixture over the cake in the bowl. Arrange remaining cake, jam side up, over the custard. Drizzle remaining sherry over cake and spoon remaining custard over top. Refrigerate at least 4 hours or overnight. Just before serving, sprinkle toasted almonds on top.

FROSTING, COCOA
(A thin, dark frosting that tastes great over cakes or cookies that do not call for a thick, creamy frosting. This is great for those confections which need just a thin layer of chocolate.)

1/3 c. cocoa	3 Tbsp. butter, softened
1 c. confectioners'	2 Tbsp. milk
sugar	1/2 tsp. vanilla

In a small bowl, mix together cocoa and confectioners' sugar. In a separate, medium bowl, cream together butter with half cocoa mixture. Alternately add remaining cocoa mixture with milk, beating until smooth. Stir in vanilla. Refrigerate until ready to use. Spread thinly over desired cakes or cookies.

FROSTING, COOKED CHOCOLATE
(This is an old-fashioned recipe that tastes just as good now as it did then. A somewhat thick frosting that is an excellent choice for frosting cakes and similar confections. This is a dark, not-too-sweet frosting.)

2 Tbsp. butter	1/2 tsp. vanilla
1 1/4 tsp. flour	1 1/2 c. confectioners' sugar
1/8 tsp. salt	1/3 c. cocoa
1/4 c. milk	

In a medium, heavy saucepan, over low heat, add butter and cook until melted. Remove pan from burner. Stir in flour and salt. Return to burner, increase heat to medium-high, and add milk. Bring to a boil. Boil 1 minute, stirring constantly. Remove from heat. Stir in vanilla, confectioners' sugar and cocoa. Stir until smooth. Pour into bowl. Refrigerate until ready to use.

DESSERTS

FROSTING, COOKED VANILLA
(Another old-fashioned recipe. After tasting these cooked frostings, and seeing how truly easy they are to make, it will be difficult to have anything other than "homemade" again.)

2 1/2 Tbsp. flour	4 Tbsp. shortening
1/2 c. milk	1/2 c. sugar (granulated)
4 Tbsp. butter, softened	1 tsp. vanilla

In a small, heavy saucepan, over medium heat, add flour and milk. Cook until thick, stirring continuously. Cool in refrigerator. In a large mixing bowl, mix together butter, shortening, sugar and vanilla. Add cooled mixture and beat until smooth. Refrigerate until ready to use.

FROSTING, CREAM CHEESE
(A delicious, creamy, easy-to-make frosting that tastes particularly great on carrot cakes or any cake made with fruit. This frosting is not-too-sweet and has a somewhat thick consistency.)

1 (8 oz.) pkg. cream cheese, softened	1 Tbsp. vanilla
2 Tbsp. butter, softened	2 c. confectioners' sugar

In a large mixing bowl, mix together cream cheese, butter and vanilla until smooth. Add confectioners' sugar and continue beating until smooth. Refrigerate until ready to use.

FROSTING, WHIPPED CREAM

(This light and fluffy frosting is just about as easy as it gets! The creamy texture is so smooth and delicious, you may want to eat just the frosting alone! You can use any kind of pudding you like, depending on the cake you will be frosting. Just think, all you have to do is change the pudding flavor and there you have it, a new frosting everytime!)

1/2 (3.4 oz.) pkg. instant pudding (any flavor)　　　**1 pt. whipping cream**

In a large mixing bowl, mix together pudding and whipping cream. Beat on high until thickened and peaks form. Refrigerate until ready to use.

FUDGE

(This is "never-fail" fudge! It is so easy-to-make and tastes so good, you will be making it all the time. This won't last long as just about everyone loves homemade fudge!)

2 c. sugar
18 marshmallows
2/3 c. evaporated milk

1 c. semi-sweet chocolate morsels
4 Tbsp. butter
1 tsp. vanilla

Butter a 9" square pan. In a medium, heavy saucepan, over medium-high heat, add sugar, marshmallows and milk. Bring to a boil, stirring constantly. Boil 6 - 7 minutes, stirring constantly. Remove from heat. Immediately add chocolate morsels, butter and vanilla. Stir until melted. Pour into prepared pan. Refrigerate until hardened. Cut into small squares.

GERMAN COOKIES

(This recipe has been around for many years and is just as good now as it was then. This is another classic example of how things seem to change so much and yet always remain the same. Enjoy this old-fashioned recipe and let it conjure up images of days-gone-by. I know I do.)

8 Tbsp. butter, softened	1 3/4 c. flour
	1/2 tsp. baking soda
1 c. dark brown sugar	1/4 tsp. salt
	1/2 c. walnuts, chopped
1 egg	(optional)

In a large mixing bowl, beat together butter, brown sugar and egg. In a separate, medium bowl, mix together flour, baking soda and salt. Add to the first mixture and mix well. Stir in nuts. Shape into a roll or rolls about 2" in diameter. Wrap in wax paper or foil and store in the refrigerator until ready to bake. (Dough will keep well for at least one week and may also be frozen.) Before baking, preheat oven to 350°. Using a sharp knife, slice in rounds 1/4" thick. Bake on ungreased cookie sheets about 10 - 12 minutes, until crisp and lightly browned. Cool 3 - 4 minutes on cookie sheets before removing to a wire rack. Serve warm or completely cooled, as desired.

THE HARRIED HOUSEWIFE SAYS....
Did you ever notice that even when women "downsize" from a larger purse to a smaller purse because they have decided they "don't need" all the "stuff" they have accumulated in their larger version, they still somehow manage to <u>cram</u> just about the same amount of "stuff" into their new, petite, pretty, little purse!

GERMAN NUT CAKE
*(A deliciously moist cake with just enough maraschino cherries
making this is a perfect example of what an old-fashioned,
homemade cake should be. Top each slice of cooled cake with a
little bit of freshly whipped cream and a slice of cherry, if desired.)*

8 Tbsp. butter,	**2 c. flour**
softened	**2 tsp. baking powder**
4 eggs	**1/2 c. walnuts, chopped**
2 c. sugar	**1/2 c. maraschino cherries**
1/2 pt. sour cream	**freshly whipped cream**
1 tsp. vanilla	**(optional)**

Preheat oven to 350°. Grease a tube (Bundt) pan. In a large mixing
bowl, mix together butter, eggs, sugar, sour cream and vanilla. Add
flour and baking powder and mix well. Stir in nuts and cherries.
Pour into prepared pan. Bake 55 - 60 minutes. Cool in pan 15
minutes. Invert onto wire rack. Cool completely. Top with freshly
whipped cream and a slice of cherry, if desired.

Tip: To see if a cake is done, the old-fashioned method of inserting
a toothpick into the center of the cake is still the best. If it comes
out clean, you will know it is done.

DESSERTS

GOLDEN CAKE

(This is the perfect "Birthday Cake." A simple, delicious, white cake which is moist and full-of-flavor. This is also a great cake to make on the spur-of-the moment as you probably already have all the necessary ingredients in your kitchen. In keeping with the old-fashioned, homemade way of doing things, frost with Frosting, Cooked Vanilla, if desired. You are sure to enjoy!)

2 1/4 c. flour	1/2 c. vegetable oil
3 tsp. baking powder	1 c. milk
1 tsp. salt	2 eggs
1 1/4 c. sugar	3 tsp. vanilla

Preheat oven to 350°. Lightly grease and flour two 8" or 9" round cake pans. In a large mixing bowl, mix together flour, baking powder, salt and sugar. Add the oil and milk and beat 2 minutes. Add eggs and vanilla and beat another 2 minutes. Pour into prepared pans and bake 25 - 30 minutes. Cool in pans 5 - 10 minutes before turning out onto wire racks. Cool completely before frosting.

Tip: While most cakes taste best when they are fresh, no more than a day or two old, if you plan to keep a cake several days, wrap in foil or plastic wrap and keep in the refrigerator. Of course, those with perishable fillings or frostings must always be refrigerated. All cakes freeze well as long as they are wrapped tightly before freezing to prevent "freezer burn" which can happen if air gets into the wrappings. To defrost cakes, remove from freezer and allow to thaw on the counter, unwrapped, 1 - 2 hours.

HALF MOONS

(A delicious, white "cookie" with one-half frosted with chocolate frosting and the other half frosted with vanilla frosting. A real party pleaser! May frost with Frosting, Cooked Chocolate and Frosting, Cooked Vanilla, if desired.)

3 c. flour	1 1/2 c. sugar
1 tsp. baking powder	2 eggs
1 tsp. baking soda	1 tsp. vanilla
1/2 tsp. salt	1 c. sour milk*
3/4 c. shortening	

Preheat oven to 375°. Lightly grease cookie sheets. In a large mixing bowl, mix together flour, baking powder, baking soda and salt. Add shortening, sugar, eggs and vanilla. Beat well. Add sour milk and mix well. Drop by tablespoonfuls onto prepared cookie sheets. Bake for 10 - 12 minutes. Cool 3 - 4 minutes before removing to wire racks. Cool completely. Frost one-half with chocolate frosting, and the other half with vanilla frosting.

*SOUR MILK

(This is the easiest way to "sour" milk!)

1 c. milk
1 Tbsp. white vinegar
  or lemon juice

Add 1 tablespoon white vinegar or 1 tablespoon lemon juice to 1 cup of milk and let stand at room temperature 10 - 15 minutes.

DESSERTS

HOT FUDGE SAUCE
(A thick, rich topping for ice-cream or your favorite dessert. This tastes better when served slightly warm. Delicious!)

1/2 c. butter
4 oz. unsweetened
  chocolate
3 c. sugar

1/2 tsp. salt
1 c. evaporated milk
1 tsp. vanilla

In a medium, heavy saucepan, over low heat, add butter and chocolate. Cook until melted, stirring continuously. Add sugar, salt and milk. Continue cooking over low heat until sugar is dissolved and mixture thickens, stirring constantly. Remove from heat. Stir in vanilla. Cool slightly before serving.

LEMONADE CAKE
(A tasty treat! Everyone will like this unique, moist and delicious cake. May frost with "Glaze," if desired.)

1 pkg. lemon cake mix
1 (3.4 oz.) pkg. instant
  lemon pudding

4 eggs
1 c. water
1/4 c. vegetable oil

Preheat oven to 350°. Lightly grease a 9" x 13" baking pan. In a large mixing bowl, mix together cake mix, pudding, eggs, water and oil. Beat well. Pour into prepared pan. Bake 45 - 50 minutes. Cool 5 minutes. With a utility fork, poke holes all over cake being sure to go all the way to the bottom of cake. Slowly pour glaze over cake until all has been absorbed.

GLAZE

2 c. confectioners' sugar

1 (6 oz.) can concentrated
  lemonade, thawed

In a medium mixing bowl, add sugar and lemonade and beat well.

LEMON SQUARES

(A delectable treat! Not too tart with just enough lemon juice to add a slightly tangy flavor. These squares are moist and delicious. They make an excellent snack as well as being a good choice to bring for a picnic or to a friend's house as they travel well. May sprinkle a little confectioners' sugar on top, if desired.)

1 c. butter, melted	2 c. granulated sugar
2 c. flour plus 4 Tbsp. flour	1 tsp. baking powder
	4 eggs
1/2 c. confectioners' sugar	6 Tbsp. fresh lemon juice
	1/4 tsp. salt

Preheat oven to 350°. In a large bowl, mix together butter, 2 cups flour and confectioners' sugar. Pat into the bottom of an ungreased 9" x 13" baking pan. Bake 15 minutes. In a large mixing bowl, mix together granulated sugar, 4 tablespoons flour and baking powder. Add eggs, lemon juice and salt and beat well. Pour mixture over hot crust. Return to oven. Bake 25 - 30 minutes. Cool completely. Cut into squares. Sprinkle confectioners' sugar on top, if desired.

Tip: *When buying lemons, look for heavy, firm (but not hard) fruit with a bright yellow color. Try to avoid coarse, thick-skinned lemons as they will yield little juice. It is a good idea to have one or two lemons in the kitchen at all times since they are readily available and keep well. You may always add a fresh slice or wedge of lemon to just about any drink, including bottled or spring water, to "freshen" it up a little. Use as a seasoning to bring out natural flavors and of course, use the juice as an aid to prevent discoloration of certain fruits and vegetables.*

MELON BOWLS WITH DRESSING

(A refreshing, easy-to-make dessert! This looks as pretty to serve as it does to eat. You may use whatever fruit you choose, depending on what is in season. A great idea for breakfast or brunch!)

1/2 c. sour cream
2 Tbsp. honey
1/2 tsp. orange peel, grated
1/4 tsp. salt
1 Tbsp. orange juice
1 tsp. lemon juice
2 honeydew melons or 2 canteloupes, halved and seeded

1 pt. fresh blueberries, stems removed, washed and gently patted dry
1 pt. fresh strawberries, washed, hulled and gently patted dry
2 bananas, sliced (just before serving)

In a medium mixing bowl, mix together sour cream and honey. Add orange peel and salt and mx well. Slowly beat in orange juice and lemon juice. Cover and chill at least 1 hour. When ready to serve, arrange blueberries, strawberries and bananas in melon bowls. Spoon dressing over all.

THE HARRIED HOUSEWIFE SAYS....
Nothing tastes better than a fresh apple, just shaken from the tree or the anticipated pleasure of a freshly picked, bright red strawberry. Fresh fruit, in all of its glorious abundance, is a simple pleasure that should never be overlooked.

MOLASSES COOKIES
(An old-fashioned favorite! These cookies have been around for many years and are still just as good now as they were then. This is an old recipe, sure to be enjoyed by everyone.)

8 Tbsp. butter, softened	**1 c. whole-wheat flour**
3/4 c. sugar	**2 tsp. baking soda**
1/2 c. dark molasses	**1 tsp. cinnamon**
1 egg	**3/4 tsp. ginger**
1 c. flour	**1/4 tsp. salt**

In a large mixing bowl, cream together butter and sugar. Add molasses and egg and beat well. In a separate, medium bowl, mix together flour, whole-wheat flour, baking soda, cinnamon, ginger and salt. Add to the first mixture and stir until well blended. Cover and refrigerate, at least 30 minutes. After dough has chilled, preheat oven to 375°. Lightly grease cookie sheets. Form dough into 1" balls. Place on prepared cookie sheets, about 2" apart. With a fork, make a crosshatch pattern on each cookie (dip fork in cold water if it sticks to dough). You may sprinkle a little extra sugar on each cookie, if desired. Place in oven and bake 10 - 12 minutes or until lightly browned. Be sure to not overbake. Cool on cookie sheets 3 - 4 minutes before removing to wire racks. Serve warm or completely cooled, as desired.

Tip: When molasses cookies have just about completely cooled, immediately wrap them or store them in a tightly-sealed container if you wish to retain a chewy consistency. Otherwise, they may become hard and crunchy.

DESSERTS

OATMEAL COOKIES

(This is a classic cookie loved by just about everyone. This recipe has been around for many years and is likely to be around for many more. You may add raisins, if desired. There aren't many things in life that compare so favorably to freshly-baked oatmeal cookies, still warm from the oven, with a nice, tall glass of milk.)

3/4 c. shortening
1 1/4 c. light brown
  sugar
1 egg
1/3 c. milk
1 tsp. vanilla

3 c. oats
1 c. flour
1/2 tsp. baking soda
1/2 tsp. salt
1/2 tsp. cinnamon

Preheat oven to 375°. Lightly grease cookie sheets. In a large mixing bowl, mix together shortening, brown sugar, egg, milk and vanilla. In a separate, large bowl, mix together oats, flour, baking soda, salt and cinnamon. Add to first mixture. Blend well. Drop by rounded tablespoons 2" apart onto prepared cooking sheets. Bake 10 - 12 minutes or until lightly browned. Cool on cookie sheets 3 - 4 minutes before removing to wire racks. Serve warm or cooled, as desired.

PEACH ANGEL CAKE

(A quick, no-bake delicious dessert!)

1 (10 oz.) angel food cake
1/2 pt. whipping cream
1/2 (3.4 oz.) pkg. instant
  vanilla pudding

1 (16 oz.) can sliced peaches,
  drained, coarsely chopped,
  4 slices reserved

Slice cake in half. In a medium mixing bowl, beat whipping cream with pudding until thickened. Add chopped peaches to mixture. Spread about 3/4 mixture on bottom half of cake. Put top layer of cake over whipped cream mixture. Spread remaining mixture on top. Slice 4 remaining peaches in half and garnish. Refrigerate until serving.

PEACH COBBLER

(A delicious, old-fashioned dessert that is a must-have when we are looking for an authentic, homemade dessert. There is hardly a better way to greet them as they walk through the door than the smell of peaches baking in the oven. This is an excellent choice for a cozy evening at home. Serve warm, with freshly whipped cream, if desired.)

1 3/4 c. sliced peaches, peeled
1 c. sugar, divided
1/4 c. water
1 egg
1 Tbsp. butter, softened

1 Tbsp. milk
1 tsp. almond extract
1/2 c. flour
1/2 tsp. baking powder
1/4 tsp. salt

Preheat oven to 375°. Butter 8" baking pan. In a medium, heavy saucepan, over medium-high heat, add peaches, 1/2 cup sugar and water. Bring to a boil, stirring occasionally. Reduce heat to low and keep warm on burner. In a large mixing bowl, mix together egg, remaining 1/2 cup sugar and butter until fluffy. Add milk and almond extract and mix well. Add flour, baking powder and salt and mix until well blended. Spread in prepared pan and pour hot peaches over all. Bake 25 - 30 minutes or until lightly browned. Cool slightly before serving. Top with freshly whipped cream, if desired.

Tip: *To peel peaches, gently place them in boiling water for just 1 - 2 minutes. Remove pan from burner and immediately remove peaches from water. Peel with a sharp knife. The skin with come off easily.*

PEANUT BUTTER COOKIES

(A timeless cookie. It is amazing how we sometimes relate memories to the food we enjoyed at that time in our lives. These particular cookies bring back fond memories of childhood. I remember my Aunt Clara always seemed to have a bottomless cookie jar. My cousin Robbie and I used to always "raid" that cookie jar. Homemade peanut butter cookies was our usual treat of the day. Of course we looked forward to when she would give them to us herself, but it was always more fun when we would "sneak" them! Enjoy these old-fashioned cookies as much as Robbie and I did, and still do.)

3/4 c. smooth peanut butter	1 egg
1/4 c. butter, softened	1 c. flour
1/4 c. shortening	1/2 tsp. baking soda
1/2 c. light brown sugar	1/4 tsp. salt

Preheat oven to 350°. In a large mixing bowl, mix together peanut butter, butter, shortening and brown sugar. Beat until smooth and fluffy. Add egg and beat well. Add flour, baking soda and salt and stir until well blended. Roll tablespoons of dough between the palms of hands to about 1 1/2" balls. Place on ungreased cookie sheets and with a fork, make a crosshatch pattern (dip fork in cold water if it sticks to dough). Bake 8 - 10 minutes. Be sure to not let them get too brown on the bottom. Cool on cookie sheets 3 - 4 minutes before removing to wire racks. Serve warm or cooled, as desired.

PEANUT BUTTER KISS COOKIES

(A delightful cookie with a "kiss" on it! These are easy-to-make and are great for a large party or to give as a small token gift around the holidays or anytime. Just about everyone likes receiving homemade treats and these are especially appreciated.)

1 3/4 c. flour
1 tsp. baking soda
1/2 tsp. salt
4 Tbsp. butter, softened
1/4 c. shortening
1/3 c. smooth peanut butter

1/2 c. sugar plus 1/4 c. sugar (to roll dough in before baking)
1/2 c. light brown sugar
1 egg
1 tsp. vanilla
chocolate kisses

Preheat oven to 350°. In a medium bowl, mix together flour, baking soda and salt. In a large mixing bowl, cream together butter, shortening and peanut butter. Add 1/2 cup granulated sugar, brown sugar, egg and vanilla to peanut butter mixture and beat well. Add dry ingredients to peanut butter mixture and stir until well blended. Roll tablespoons of dough between the palms of hands to about 1 1/2" balls. Roll in remaining 1/4 cup sugar. Place on ungreased cookie sheets and with a fork, make a crosshatch pattern (dip fork in cold water if it sticks to dough). Bake 8 minutes. Remove from oven and place a chocolate kiss firmly on each. Bake another 2 minutes. Cool on cookie sheets 3 - 4 minutes before removing to wire racks. Serve warm or cooled, as desired.

DESSERTS

PEANUT CLUSTERS

(These tasty treats are great to have when company drops by. They make a nice "thank-you" gift for someone special as they are a delicious cross between a candy and a cookie. A nice change!)

1 c. sugar
4 Tbsp. butter
1/3 c. evaporated milk
1/4 c. chunky peanut
  butter

1/2 tsp. vanilla
1 c. oats
1/2 c. Spanish peanuts

Lightly oil a large piece of wax paper. In a medium, heavy saucepan, over medium-high heat, add sugar, butter and milk. Bring to a boil. Boil 3 minutes, stirring constantly. Remove from heat. Immediately stir in peanut butter and vanilla. Fold in oats and peanuts. Drop by tablespoonfuls onto prepared wax paper. Let stand until set.

PEANUT COOKIES

(Another delicious, unique cookie that resembles candy. A great gift idea.)

2 egg whites
1/2 c. sugar
1 c. peanuts, chopped
  (unsalted)

2 tsp. vanilla

Preheat oven to 300°. Grease cookie sheets. In a medium mixing bowl, beat egg whites until stiff. Gradually add sugar, beating constantly. Stir in peanuts and vanilla. Drop by teaspoonfuls onto prepared cookie sheets, about 2" apart. Bake 12 - 15 minutes. Cool on cookie sheets 3 - 4 minutes before removing to wire racks. Cool completely before serving.

PECAN PIE

(This delectable, sweet, dark pie is a must-have for holiday entertaining. Of course, it is so easy-to-make and they enjoy it so much, it is a natural choice for dessert any night of the week. Serve warm, topped with plenty of freshly whipped cream, if desired.)

pastry dough for 9"	**1/4 tsp. salt**
one-crust pie	**1 c. dark corn syrup**
3 eggs, lightly beaten	**1 tsp. vanilla**
3/4 c. sugar	**1 c. pecan halves**

Preheat oven to 425°. Line pie pan with pastry dough. In a large mixing bowl, mix together eggs, sugar, salt, corn syrup and vanilla. Stir in pecans. Pour into prepared pan. Bake 10 minutes. Reduce heat to 350°. Bake another 35 minutes. Serve warm or completely cooled, as desired. Top with freshly whipped cream, if desired.

PIE CRUST (TWO 9" PIE SHELLS)

(If I can make pie crust, so can you! This is the easiest way to do it and it always turns out great. You should be proud of yourself, turning out a real, homemade pie with genuine pie crust made from your very own hands. I'm proud of you, too!)

2 c. flour	**1 c. shortening**
1/2 tsp. salt	**6 - 7 Tbsp. ice water**

In a medium bowl, mix together flour and salt. Cut in shortening with a pastry blender or two knives (a fork will do). Combine lightly only until mixture resembles coarse meal or very tiny peas. Sprinkle water over mixture, 1 tablespoon at a time, and mix lightly with a fork, using only enough water so the dough will hold together when pressed gently into a ball. Make 2 balls. Chill 15 minutes. On a lightly-floured surface, roll dough out 2" larger than the pie pan. Fit it loosely but firmly into the pan. Fill with desired filling. Roll out other ball. Place on top of filling. Crimp or flute edges. Bake as directed according to the filling recipe.

DESSERTS

PISTACHIO CAKE

(This is an annual favorite at our house on St. Patrick's Day. Everyone knows this is a "sure bet" when they stop by to help us celebrate this festive occasion! Of course, it doesn't usually last long as there is always quite a crowd! This cake is about as moist as you could ever ask for with an equally delicious frosting that complements this outstanding cake. The best part is, it is so easy-to-make, and tastes as if you spent hours on it. They will never know the truth!)

1 pkg. vanilla cake mix	4 eggs
1 (3.4 oz.) pkg. instant pistachio pudding	1 c. water
	1/4 c. vegetable oil
	3 - 4 drops green food color (optional)

Preheat oven to 350°. Lightly grease a 9" x 13" baking pan. In a large mixing bowl, combine all ingredients. Beat at medium speed 4 minutes. Pour into prepared pan. Bake 45 - 50 minutes. Cool completely before frosting.

FROSTING

(A delectable, light and creamy frosting.)

1/2 (3.4 oz.) pkg. instant pistachio pudding	5 - 6 drops green food color (optional)
1 pt. whipping cream	

In a medium mixing bowl, combine pudding and whipping cream. Beat until slightly thickened. Add food color. Continue beating until thickened and peaks form. Cover and refrigerate until ready to use.

POPCORN BALLS
(These were always standard fare at our house on Halloween! All the kids in the neighborhood knew it and made sure our house was one of their "first stops" when trick-or-treating! Lucky for them, there was always plenty to go around. Bless my mother's heart!)

3 qts. popped corn, unbuttered and unsalted	1 Tbsp. cider vinegar
	1/4 tsp. salt
	2 tsp. vanilla
2 c. light corn syrup	

Butter a large bowl and a large spoon. Put popcorn in buttered bowl and keep warm in a 250° oven. In a heavy saucepan, combine the corn syrup, vinegar and salt. Cook over medium heat, stirring occasionally, until the syrup reaches the hard-ball stage (250°F). Remove from heat and add vanilla. Slowly pour the syrup over popcorn, stirring with buttered spoon to coat each kernel. As soon as the mixture is cool enough to handle, quickly and gently shape into 3" balls (you may need to butter your hands). Place popcorn balls on wax paper until they are cool and no longer sticky, then wrap each in plastic wrap. Store at room temperature.

THE HARRIED HOUSEWIFE SAYS....
Did you ever notice that when you "vacation" with children, when you come home you need a vacation from "vacation!"

DESSERTS

POPPY SEED COFFEE CAKE
(This cake is moist and full-of-flavor with just enough nuts, rendering a slightly coarse texture. This would be an excellent choice for an afternoon tea as well as rounding out the table for a Sunday brunch. It is also great to bring to someone's house when you are not quite sure what to bring, as it can be enjoyed so many different ways.)

2 c. sugar	1 1/2 tsp. baking powder
1 1/2 c. vegetable oil	1/4 tsp. salt
4 eggs	1/4 c. poppy seeds
1 tsp. vanilla	1 (12 oz.) can evaporated milk
3 c. flour	1 c. walnuts, chopped

Preheat oven to 325°. Lightly grease tube (Bundt) pan. In a large mixing bowl, mix together sugar, oil, eggs and vanilla. In a separate, medium bowl, mix together flour, baking powder and salt. Add to the first mixture and blend well. Alternately add poppy seeds, milk and walnuts. Stir just to blend. Pour into prepared pan. Bake 1 - 1 1/2 hours or until toothpick inserted in center comes out clean. Cool in pan 15 minutes. Invert onto a wire rack. Cool completely before serving.

THE HARRIED HOUSWIFE SAYS....
It never fails to happen that the second you finally sit down to enjoy a long-awaited cup of hot, fresh coffee and a leisurely "look" at the newspaper, the phone rings with a long-distance call from your long-lost relative who decides to fill you in on every detail of her life for the past 10 years! And isn't worried about the phone bill, to boot!

POUND CAKE

(This is a moist, heavy, not-too-sweet cake flavored with just the right amount of lemon and the rich flavor of butter. Enjoy this delectable cake alone or topped with fresh fruit.)

3 c. flour	1/2 c. shortening
1/4 tsp. salt	2 tsp. vanilla
5 eggs	1/2 tsp. lemon extract
3 c. sugar	1 c. lemon-lime soda
3/4 c. butter, softened	

Preheat oven to 325°. Grease tube (Bundt) pan. In a medium bowl, mix together flour and salt. In a large mixing bowl, mix together eggs, sugar, butter, shortening, vanilla, extract and soda. Beat on medium speed until light and fluffy, about 4 - 5 minutes. Reduce speed to low and add dry ingredients and soda, alternately, beginning and ending with dry ingredients. Bake 1 - 1 1/2 hours or until toothpick inserted in center comes out clean. Cool in pan 15 minutes. Invert onto wire rack. Cool completely before serving.

THE HARRIED HOUSEWIFE SAYS....
Isn't it ironic that on the day your cupboards happen to be filled to capacity (with newly purchased Tupperware and kitchen gadgets you "had to have") that someone comes over and decides to "help" herself to a cup of coffee. Of course, in her quest for a cup, she opens up every cupboard and undoubtedly gets "clunked" on the head by all the kitchen paraphernalia that comes tumbling out after you strategically "shoved" everything in there and quickly slammed the door shut!

DESSERTS

PUMPKIN PIE
(This is probably one of the first things we think of when we think about the holidays. A timeless pie, this is a classic favorite. Nothing says homemade and old-fashioned as much as a creamy, warm pumpkin pie topped with plenty of whipped cream and a sprinkle of cinnamon. Enjoy this traditional recipe and let it help you conjure up images of cozy days-gone-by and help you dream of pleasant days-to-come.)

pastry dough for 9"
  one-crust pie
1 (16 oz.) can
  pumpkin
1 (14 oz.) can sweetened
  condensed milk

2 eggs
1 1/2 tsp. cinnamon
1/2 tsp. ginger
1/2 tsp. salt

Preheat oven to 425°. Line a pie pan with pastry dough. In a large mixing bowl, mix together all ingredients. Pour into lined pan. Bake 15 minutes. Reduce oven to 350° and bake 40 - 45 minutes or until knife inserted near center comes out clean. Serve warm or completely cooled, as desired.

Tip: Placing a beautiful and bountiful bowl of fruit in the middle of the table makes a practical and pretty centerpiece. Select different varieties of fruit depending on what's in season and look for nice shapes and contrasting colors that will make an attractive composition. Polish apples and pears until they shine. Add a surprising touch like a sprinkling of bright berries. A contrast of dried fruits and nuts is a good idea as well, especially during winter months.

RASPBERRY PIE

(This is a delightful, fresh-tasting pie that boasts of delectable, fresh, raspberries and is full of home-spun appeal. It is easy-to-make and tastes so good, it is sure to become a favorite.)

pastry dough for 9"   **1 qt. fresh raspberries, divided**
  one-crust pie   **3/4 c. sugar**
3 Tbsp. cornstarch   **3 Tbsp. lemon juice**
1/2 c. water, divided   **topping***

Preheat oven to 425°. Line a pie pan with pastry dough and prick all over with a fork. Bake 12 - 15 minutes or until light brown. Remove from oven and cool. In a medium bowl, dissolve cornstarch in 1/4 cup of water. Set aside. In a medium saucepan, combine 2 cups of raspberries, remaining water, sugar and lemon juice. Bring to a boil. Remove 2 tablespoons of berry mixture and mix with the cornstarch. Return to the saucepan. Cook 1 minute, stirring constantly. Mixture will be thick. Refrigerate until serving. Just before serving, add remaining 2 cups raspberries to mixture and gently stir. Pour filling into pie crust. Spread Topping over pie. Serve immediately.

*TOPPING
(This is your basic, freshly whipped cream topping that can go on just about anything and always adds that highly desired "homemade" flair.)

1/2 pt. whipping cream   **1/4 tsp. vanilla**
1 tsp. sugar

In a medium mixing bowl, beat together all ingredients until thickened and peaks form. Spread on pie.

DESSERTS

REFRIGERATOR COOKIES

(A delightful, old-fashioned cookie that has been around for many years. The nice thing about these cookies is that you can make the dough ahead of time and refrigerate or freeze it until ready to use. This comes in handy on those rare occasions when we happen to have just a little extra time and can actually make cookie dough ahead of time to use in the near future. Doesn't it feel great to be so organized?!)

8 Tbsp. butter,	**1 egg**
softened	**1 1/2 c. flour**
1 tsp. vanilla	**1/2 tsp. cream of tartar**
2/3 c. brown sugar	**1/4 tsp. salt**
1/3 c. sugar	

In a large mixing bowl, mix together butter and vanilla. Add both sugars and egg and beat well. In a medium bowl, mix together flour, cream of tartar and salt. Add to the first mixture and combine well. Shape into a roll or rolls about 2" in diameter. Wrap in plastic wrap or foil and store in the refrigerator until ready to bake. (Dough will keep well for at least one week and may also be frozen.) Before baking, preheat oven to 400°. Using a sharp knife, slice in rounds 1/4" thick. Bake on ungreased cookie sheets 8 - 10 minutes, until lightly browned. Cool 3 - 4 minutes on cookie sheets before removing to wire racks. Serve warm or completely cooled, as desired.

Tip: Always bake cookies in a preheated oven unless otherwise specified. Use two cookie sheets at the same time only if your oven is wide enough to accomodate them on the same rack. The cookie sheet(s) should be on the center rack, allowing room for heat to circulate around it, unless the recipe specifies otherwise. Also, allow cookie sheets to cool off a little before putting new cookies on them, or the next batch may not hold their shapes.

RICE PUDDING

(It doesn't get much easier than this! Homemade rice pudding in just a few minutes! This delightful, creamy pudding will have them believing you worked so hard just for them. They will never know!)

4 c. milk	1 egg, beaten
1 c. instant rice	1/2 c. raisins (optional)
1 (3.4 oz.) pkg.	1/2 tsp. cinnamon
vanilla pudding	1/4 tsp. nutmeg

In a heavy saucepan, over medium-high heat, combine together milk, rice, pudding, egg and raisins. Cook until mixture comes to a boil, stirring continuously. Remove from heat. Cover and let stand 5 minutes, stirring twice. Pour into dessert dishes or serving bowl. Sprinkle with cinnamon and nutmeg. Serve warm.

RUM BALLS

(An excellent gift idea! Place these delicious little treats in a pretty, tightly-sealed glass container and tie with a beautiful ribbon. They will definitely appreciate your thoughtfulness and delight in being on the receiving end of your good taste.)

2 c. vanilla wafer	2 Tbsp. light corn syrup
crumbs	1/2 c. Rum
1 c. coconut	
2 1/2 c. confectioners'	
sugar, separated	

In a large bowl, mix together crumbs, coconut, 1 cup of confectioners' sugar, corn syrup and rum. Shape into small, firm balls, 1" in diameter. Sift the remaining 1 1/2 cups confectioners' sugar onto a piece of wax paper. Roll the balls in the sugar. Store in a tightly-sealed container until needed.

DESSERTS

RUM CAKE

(A moist, heavy cake with the distinct flavor of Rum. A delightful cake which is a great choice to make for company as well as being an excellent treat to bring to someone's house. Topped with your choice of pecans or walnuts with a light glaze of butter and rum, this cake is as appealing to the eyes as it is to the tastebuds. Enjoy!)

1 c. pecans or walnuts, chopped
1 pkg. yellow cake mix
1 (3.4 oz) pkg. instant vanilla pudding

4 eggs
1/2 c. water
1/2 c. vegetable oil
1/2 c. Dark Rum
glaze*

Preheat oven to 325°. Grease and flour a tube (Bundt) pan. Sprinkle nuts on bottom of pan. In a large mixing bowl, add all remaining cake ingredients and mix well. Pour batter over nuts. Bake 55 - 60 minutes or until toothpick inserted in center comes out clean. Cool 5 minutes. Invert onto serving plate. With a utility fork, poke holes all over cake being sure to go all the way to the bottom of cake. Slowly pour glaze evenly over cake as well as brushing on sides. Allow cake to absorb glaze. Cool completely before serving.

*GLAZE
(A sweet, buttery glaze with the distinct flavor of Rum.)

8 Tbsp. butter
1/4 c. water

1 c. sugar
1/2 c. Dark Rum

In a medium, heavy saucepan, over medium heat, add butter and melt. Stir in water and sugar. Bring to a boil and boil 5 minutes, stirring continuously. Remove from heat. Stir in rum. Pour warm glaze over slightly cooled cake.

SHORTBREAD

(Another classic cookie. A timeless favorite which has been around for many years and is enjoyed just as much now as it was then. Enjoy this old-fashioned, slightly crumbly, buttery cookie. It will bring you back.)

1/2 pound butter, softened	2 c. flour
1/2 c. confectioners' sugar	1/2 tsp. salt
	1/4 tsp. baking powder

Preheat oven to 350°. In a large mixing bowl, beat together butter and sugar. In a separate, medium bowl, mix together flour, salt and baking powder. Add to the first mixture, combining thoroughly. Roll out the dough with a rolling pin until it is 1/4" thick. Cut into rectangles. Place on ungreased cookie sheets and prick each cookie with a fork. Bake 20 - 25 minutes or until lightly browned around the edges. Cool 3 - 4 minutes on cookie sheets before removing to wire racks. Serve warm or completely cooled, as desired.

THE HARRIED HOUSEWIFE SAYS....
Be sure to carve enough time into your busy day to sit back and relax with a cup of coffee and think about where you have been, where you are, and where you would like to be.

DESSERTS

STRAWBERRY PIE

(A delicious, fresh strawberry pie that is so easy-to-make and is full of old-fashioned, homemade flavor, you will be making this many times over. Top with freshly whipped cream, if desired.)

pastry dough for 9"
  one-crust pie
1 qt. strawberries,
  washed, hulled and
  drained

1 1/2 c. water
3/4 c. sugar
2 Tbsp. cornstarch
1 (3 oz.) pkg. strawberry jello

Preheat oven to 425°. Line pie pan with pastry dough and prick all over with a fork. Bake 12 - 15 minutes or until light brown. Cool. Arrange strawberries in cooled pie crust. In a medium, heavy saucepan, over medium-high heat, add water, sugar and cornstarch. Bring to a boil, stirring constantly, until mixture is clear. Remove from heat. Stir in jello until it dissolves. Pour over strawberries. Refrigerate until firmly set. Top with freshly whipped cream, if desired.

Tip: Wash strawberries in cold water, if necessary, and hull them after washing so they don't get soggy, unless you wish to serve them unhulled in a fruit bowl or to dip in sugar or chocolate. Be sure to wash them shortly before eating, otherwise they may soften.

...

SUGAR COOKIES

(A traditional, sugar cookie with the rich flavor of butter. You would almost want to call this cookie a butter cookie except it's just a little too crispy to be a butter cookie. Either way, this old-fashioned favorite is sure to please.)

8 Tbsp. butter, softened	1 Tbsp. milk
3/4 c. sugar	1 1/4 c. flour
1 egg	1/8 tsp. salt
1 tsp. vanilla	1/4 tsp. baking powder

Preheat oven to 350°. In a large mixing bowl, beat together butter and sugar. Add egg, vanilla and milk and beat well. In a separate, medium bowl, mix together flour, salt and baking powder. Add to the first mixture and stir until thoroughly blended. Drop by teaspoonfuls onto ungreased cookie sheets, 1" apart. Bake 8 - 10 minutes or until lightly browned. Cool 3 - 4 minutes on cookie sheets before removing to wire racks. Serve warm or completely cooled, as desired.

SWEET POTATO PIE

(A simplistic, traditional recipe. Enjoy!)

pastry dough for 9" one-crust pie	2 eggs, lightly beaten
2 c. cooked, mashed sweet potatoes	1 tsp. vanilla
	1 tsp. lemon juice
1 c. evaporated milk	1 tsp. cinnamon
1 c. sugar	1/2 tsp. nutmeg
6 Tbsp. butter, melted	1/4 tsp. salt

Preheat oven to 425°. Line pie pan with pastry dough. In a large mixing bowl, mix together all ingredients. Pour into lined pan. Bake 15 minutes. Reduce heat to 350°. Bake 40 - 45 minutes or until knife inserted near center comes out clean. Cool before serving. Top with freshly whipped cream, if desired.

DESSERTS

VANILLA FRUIT TART

(This is a unique, not-too-sweet dessert ideal for a small party. A delicious crust covered with a creamy filling made with just enough vanilla to complement the fresh fruit topping. You may use any kind of fruit you wish, depending on what is in season and your personal choice. When ready to serve, slice as you would pizza. Enjoy this heavenly treat!)

3/4 c. butter, softened	1 1/2 c. flour
1/2 c. confectioners'	vanilla filling*
sugar	fruit topping*

Preheat oven to 300°. In a large mixing bowl, beat together butter and sugar until light and fluffy. Blend in flour. Press mixture onto bottom and up side of 12" round pizza pan. Bake 20 - 25 minutes or until lightly browned. Cool. Prepare vanilla filling and spread on cooled crust. Refrigerate. Prepare Fruit Topping according to directions. Refrigerate completely assembled tart at least 1 hour before serving.

*VANILLA FILLING

1 (10 oz.) pkg. vanilla	1 (8 oz.) pkg. cream cheese,
milk chips	softened
1/2 c. whipping cream	

In a medium, heavy saucepan, over low heat, add milk chips and whipping cream and cook until chips are melted and mixture is smooth, stirring constantly. Cool. In a medium mixing bowl, add cream cheese and cooled mixture. Beat until smooth. Spread on cooled crust.

*FRUIT TOPPING

1/4 c. sugar
1 Tbsp. cornstarch
1/2 c. pineapple juice

1/2 tsp. lemon juice
assorted fresh fruit (peaches,
  kiwi, strawberries, grapes...)

In a small, heavy saucepan, over medium heat, combine together sugar and cornstarch. Stir in juices. Cook, stirring constantly, until thickened. Cool. Meanwhile, slice and arrange fresh fruit on top of filling. Pour juice mixture over fruit. Refrigerate at least 1 hour before serving.

YOGURT AND JELLO DELIGHT
(A refreshing, pretty dessert that can be made quickly and tastes delicious. It is a light dessert that goes particularly well during the summer months and would be great to top off a backyard barbecue. Use whatever kind of jello and yogurt you prefer, just as long as they are the same flavor.)

1 (3 oz.) pkg. fruit
  flavored jello

1 c. yogurt (same flavor as
  jello)

Prepare jello according to package directions. Refrigerate until it begins to set. Stir in yogurt until thoroughly combined with jello. Pour into dessert dishes or serving bowl. Refrigerate until set. Top with fresh fruit, if desired.

DESSERTS

ZUCCHINI COOKIES
(This is a great way to use fresh zucchini. These cookies are exceptionally delicious. They are chewy, with chocolate morsels that are just slightly melted, and have enough walnuts to add the right amount of crunch. Just a touch of cinnamon brings it all together. Sprinkle confectioners' sugar on top, if desired.)

8 Tbsp. butter,
  softened
1/4 c. shortening
1 1/2 c. sugar
1 egg
1 tsp. vanilla
3 - 4 drops green
  food color (optional)
1 1/2 c. zucchini,
  grated

2 1/2 c. flour
2 tsp. baking powder
2 tsp. cinnamon
1/2 tsp. salt
1/2 c. walnuts, chopped
3/4 c. semi-sweet chocolate
  morsels
1/2 c. confectioners' sugar
  (optional)

Preheat oven to 350°. Lightly grease cookie sheets. In a large mixing bowl, beat together butter, shortening and sugar until light and fluffy. Add egg, vanilla and food color. Beat well. Stir in zucchini. Add flour, baking powder, cinnamon and salt and gently stir. Add nuts and chocolate morsels. Mix until just blended. Drop by tablespoonfuls onto prepared cookie sheets. Bake 15 - 20 minutes or until lightly browned. Cool on cookie sheets 3 - 4 minutes before removing to wire racks. When completely cooled, sprinkle confectioners' sugar on top, if desired.

ZUCCHINI WHISKEY CAKE

(A moist, heavy cake with just enough whiskey to lend a slightly distinctive flavor. Filled with raisins and walnuts and just a hint of cinnamon, this cake comes alive with freshly-grated lemon zest. A truly delightful cake, you needn't even frost, as it certainly tastes great on its own. However, if you choose to frost it, Cream Cheese Frosting is a terrific choice as it will complement this delicious cake.)

1/2 c. raisins	2 eggs
1/3 c. Rye whiskey	1/2 c. vegetable oil
2 1/2 c. flour	1 1/2 c. sugar
2 tsp. baking powder	2 c. zucchini, grated
1 tsp. baking soda	1 c. walnuts, chopped
1/2 tsp. salt	2 tsp. lemon zest, freshly grated
2 tsp. cinnamon	

Preheat oven to 350°. Grease a tube (Bundt) pan. Soak the raisins in the whiskey for 10 minutes. In a medium mixing bowl, mix together flour, baking powder, baking soda, salt and cinnamon. In a large mixing bowl, mix together eggs, oil and sugar. Add raisin mixture, zucchini, nuts and zest. Mix well. Add flour mixture. Stir until thoroughly mixed. Pour batter into prepared pan. Bake 50 - 55 minutes or until toothpick inserted in center comes out clean. Cool in pan 10 minutes before turning out onto a wire rack. When completely cooled, frost with Cream Cheese Frosting and garnish with freshly-grated lemon zest, if desired.

THE HARRIED HOUSEWIFE SAYS....
It's a good idea to always have plenty of whiskey on hand as you never know when you are going to need it!

BEVERAGES

BEVERAGES

AMARETTO SLUSH
(A cool, refreshing, delicious drink which tastes great anytime. However, this is a "must-have" on those long, hot summer days. This needs to freeze overnight so be sure to plan ahead!)

1 c. sugar
4 1/2 water
1 (6 oz.) can frozen
lemonade concentrate,
thawed

1 c. Amaretto
lemon-lime soda, chilled
maraschino cherries (optional)

In a medium heavy saucepan, over medium heat, combine together sugar and water. Bring to a boil, stirring constantly, being certain sugar has dissolved. Reduce heat and simmer 15 minutes, stirring occasionally. Cool. In a large bowl, mix together lemonade and Amaretto. Add cooled mixture. Stir well. Cover and freeze mixture overnight. When ready to serve, break frozen mixture into chunks. Scoop into glasses and fill halfway. Add soda and stir until slushy. Top each with a maraschino cherry, if desired.

BANANA DAIQUIRI
(A light and refreshing drink that is full-of-flavor.)

1 banana, peeled
1 c. crushed ice
1/2 c. frozen pine
passion-banana juice
concentrate, thawed

1/4 c. water
1 oz. Rum
1 oz. orange liqueur

Put all ingredients into a blender and puree until slushy. Garnish with lime slice, if desired.

HOT COCOA

(This is true homemade hot cocoa. You have to beat it well but nothing tops the bubbly, frothy goodness derived from spending the little extra time it takes. It absolutely calls out for freshly whipped cream on top with even a sprinkle of cinnamon. This old-fashioned, delightful drink is sure to bring you back. Enjoy it now as much as you did then.)

4 Tbsp. cocoa	1/2 c. water
2 Tbsp. sugar	4 c. milk
1/8 tsp. salt	1 tsp. vanilla

In a medium, heavy saucepan, over medium heat, combine together cocoa, sugar, salt and water. Bring to a boil. Gently boil 2 minutes, stirring continuously. Add milk and heat slowly, just to the boiling point. Remove from heat. Pour into a large bowl and add vanilla. Beat well until frothy. Pour into cups and top with freshly whipped cream and a sprinkle of cinnamon, if desired. Serve immediately.

IRISH COFFEE

(My favorite! It doesn't get any better than this! There is nothing better than topping off a delicious, homemade meal with a good, old-fashioned cup of Irish Coffee! It certainly complements just about any dessert or can be enjoyed on its own. Top with plenty of freshly whipped cream, if desired. Erin-Go-Bragh!)

2 oz. Irish whiskey	1 c. very hot, strong coffee
1 tsp. sugar	

Pour whiskey into the bottom of a mug. Stir in the sugar and add piping hot, strong coffee. Top with freshly whipped cream, if desired. Serve immediately.

MAI TAI

(You don't have to go to Hawaii to enjoy the luscious, tropical taste of the islands! With a little imagination and this drink in hand, you will find yourself on a pearly-white beach somewhere in the South Pacific!)

1 c. pine-passion-banana
  juice
2 oz. Rum
1 oz. orange liqueur

1/2 tsp. almond extract
2 tsp. lime juice
cracked ice

Combine all ingredients in a glass. Serves 1.

MOCHA MIX

(This is just the thing to make for unexpected company! A rich, flavorful hot beverage with the creaminess of homemade hot cocoa with just enough coffee flavor to add a unique, delicious flavor. Make this mixture ahead of time and store in an airtight jar. When they want something other than coffee or tea, this is just right.)

2 c. coffee creamer
2 c. powdered milk
2 c. sugar

1 c. cocoa
1/4 c. instant coffee

In a large bowl, mix together all ingredients. Pour into airtight jar. When ready to use, place 2 rounded teaspoonfuls into a cup. Add boiling water and stir. Top with freshly whipped cream and a sprinkle of cocoa, if desired. Serve immediately.

BEVERAGES

OPEN HOUSE PUNCH
(This punch has a little bit of a "kick" to it! It is not-too-sweet and is just the thing to serve for an evening get-together. Add some tasty hors d'oeuvres to go along with it and you're all set! Just be sure your guests don't get a little too "tipsy" and try to drive home! That's what the couch is there for! Have a great time!)

ice
1 (6 oz.) bottle lemon
  juice
1 (6 oz.) can frozen
  orange juice,
  partially thawed

1 (6 oz.) can frozen lemonade
  concentrate, partially thawed
1/5 Southern Comfort
3 qts. lemon-lime soda

In a large punch bowl, combine all ingredients, adding soda just before serving. Add sliced orange and lemon slices, if desired.

ORANGE JULIUS
(A light and refreshing drink perfect for any occasion. This creamy drink is a favorite for both children and adults alike. It's easy-to-make and they will be happily surprised when you whip them up such a tasty treat. It's hard to believe you can make something so good so fast!)

1 (6 oz.) can frozen
  orange juice
1 c. milk
1 c. water

1/2 c. sugar
1 tsp. vanilla
5 - 6 ice cubes

Put all ingredients into a blender. Blend for 30 seconds or until slushy. Garnish with orange slice, if desired.

ORANGE MARGARITA
(This will probably be one of your favorite drinks. The orange flavor is superior. This is a great drink to quickly whip up when your friends stop by. This particular recipe makes two servings but if a few more stop by, you can certainly make more! You better stay close to the blender!)

1 c. ice	2 oz. Tequila
1 c. water	1 oz. orange liqueur
3/4 c. orange juice	1 oz. Rum

Put all ingredients into a blender and puree until slushy. Garnish with orange slice, if desired.

PEACH COOLER
(This is just the drink you need on those hot, summer days! The gentle flavor of peach is a small reminder of why peaches are so well-liked. This recipe is enough for one drink, but of course you will probably need to make more as, chances are, you will probably be enjoying such a delightful, refreshing drink with friends. Have fun!)

cracked ice	1 Tbsp. Rum
1 c. orange juice	1 Tbsp. orange liqueur
1 Tbsp. Peach Schnapps	

Combine all ingredients in a glass and stir. Garnish with unpeeled peach slice, if desired.

PEACH CUP

(The smell of peaches mixed with brown sugar and cinnamon. It doesn't get any better. And just as good as it smells cooking, is as good as it tastes. Serve this drink warm and enjoy the home-spun appeal of the flavor of peach.)

1 (40 oz.) bottle	2 cinnamon sticks (optional)
peach juice	2 Tbsp. butter
1/4 c. brown sugar	1/2 c. Peach Schnapps

In a medium, heavy saucepan, over medium-high heat, mix together juice, brown sugar, cinnamon and butter. Bring to a boil. Remove from heat. Add Schnapps. Pour into cups. Serve immediately.

PEACH DAIQUIRI

(One delicious drink! A refreshing, cool drink filled with the delicate flavor of peach. This is so smooth and tasty, you will want another! As long as you aren't going anywhere, why not live a little!)

3 medium peaches	1/4 c. Peach Schnapps or peach
or 1 (29 oz.) can	nectar
peach halves, drained	1 c. ice cubes
1/3 c. Light Rum	mint sprigs (optional)

Peel and pit peaches, reserving a few unpeeled slices for garnish, if desired. In a blender add peaches, Rum, Peach Schnapps and ice cubes. Puree until slushy. Garnish with unpeeled peach slices and mint sprigs, if desired.

RASPBERRY CHAMPAGNE PUNCH

(This is another most-requested recipe. Once you try it, you will know why. It is absolutely out-of-this world! The raspberries make this punch and the sherbet and champagne just add to the excitement! It not only tastes delicious but looks pretty as well. You will be proud to serve this luscious punch at your next gathering. Enjoy!)

2 (10 oz.) pkgs. frozen
 red raspberries in
 syrup, thawed
1/2 c. lemon juice
1/2 c. sugar

1 (750 ml) bottle red wine,
 chilled
1 qt. raspberry sherbet
1 (750 ml) bottle champagne,
 chilled

In a blender, puree raspberries. In a large punch bowl, combine raspberries, lemon juice, sugar and wine. Stir until sugar dissolves. Just before serving, scoop sherbet into punch bowl and add champagne. Stir gently. Make an ice-mold of half raspberry juice, half water and raspberries. Float in punch bowl, if desired.

RASPBERRY COOLER

(A non-alcoholic punch that is delicious and refreshing. When having a big party, why not make two bowls of punch, one with alcohol such as Raspberry Champagne Punch and this delightful counterpart! They will be truly impressed and everyone will enjoy the fresh flavor of raspberry.)

ice
1 (40 oz.) bottle
 raspberry juice, chilled
1 (32 oz.) bottle lemon
 lime soda, chilled

1 (10 oz.) pkg. frozen
 raspberries, thawed
1 (6 oz.) can frozen lemonade
 concentrate, thawed
1 lemon, thinly sliced

In a large punch bowl, combine all ingredients. Make an ice-mold of half raspberry juice, half water and raspberries. Float in punch bowl in place of ice, if desired.

SANGRIA

(A light, fruity, refreshing drink everyone will enjoy. This is appealing to the eye as it has plenty of fresh fruit floating amidst a colorful background of orange/red goodness. They will probably want to "help themselves" as they can try to "pick out" which fruit is their favorite to enjoy along with their drink! Of course, you may add whatever fruit you choose. Many folks enjoy cherries, but whatever you decide, they are sure to have a lot of fun! This is the way to entertain.)

ice
1 qt. orange juice
3 qts. red wine
2 oranges, sliced
4 fresh peaches,
  peeled and sliced

1 lemon, sliced
1 lime sliced
1/2 c. confectioners' sugar
1 qt. club soda

In a large punch bowl, combine all ingredients. Stir well. Make an ice-mold of half orange juice, half water and whatever fruits you chose for the punch. Float in punch bowl in place of ice, if desired.

STRAWBERRY MARGARITA

(One of my all-time favorites! If you like margaritas, this one is for you. It is easy-to-make and the fresh strawberries are such a treat! You can easily whip this up for company and they will love you forever! Enjoy!)

1 pt. strawberries,
  washed and hulled
  (a few reserved for
  garnish)
1/3 c. Tequila

1/4 c. fresh lime juice
1/4 c. Triple Sec or orange
  juice
2 Tbsp. sugar
1 c. ice cubes

Put all ingredients into a blender and puree until slushy. Garnish with strawberries, if desired.

WEDDING PUNCH

(This is a popular punch. It is extraordinarily creamy and is absolutely delicious. Of course it is not intended exclusively for "weddings" but makes a great punch for a child's birthday party. For whatever occasion you decide to make this, you will be pleased.)

2 1/2 c. pineapple juice, chilled
1 pt. lemon, lime or raspberry sherbet

1 pt. vanilla ice-cream, divided
1 (16 oz.) bottle lemon-lime soda

In a punch bowl, add pineapple juice, sherbet and half pint vanilla ice-cream. Stir until just smooth (a big, wooden spoon works best!). Add lemon-lime soda. Spoon remaining ice-cream into punch. Serve immediately.

THE HARRIED HOUSEWIFE SAYS....

Make a memory. It has to last,

for time has a way of going too fast.

Live each day like there is no other,

and most importantly, take care of each other.

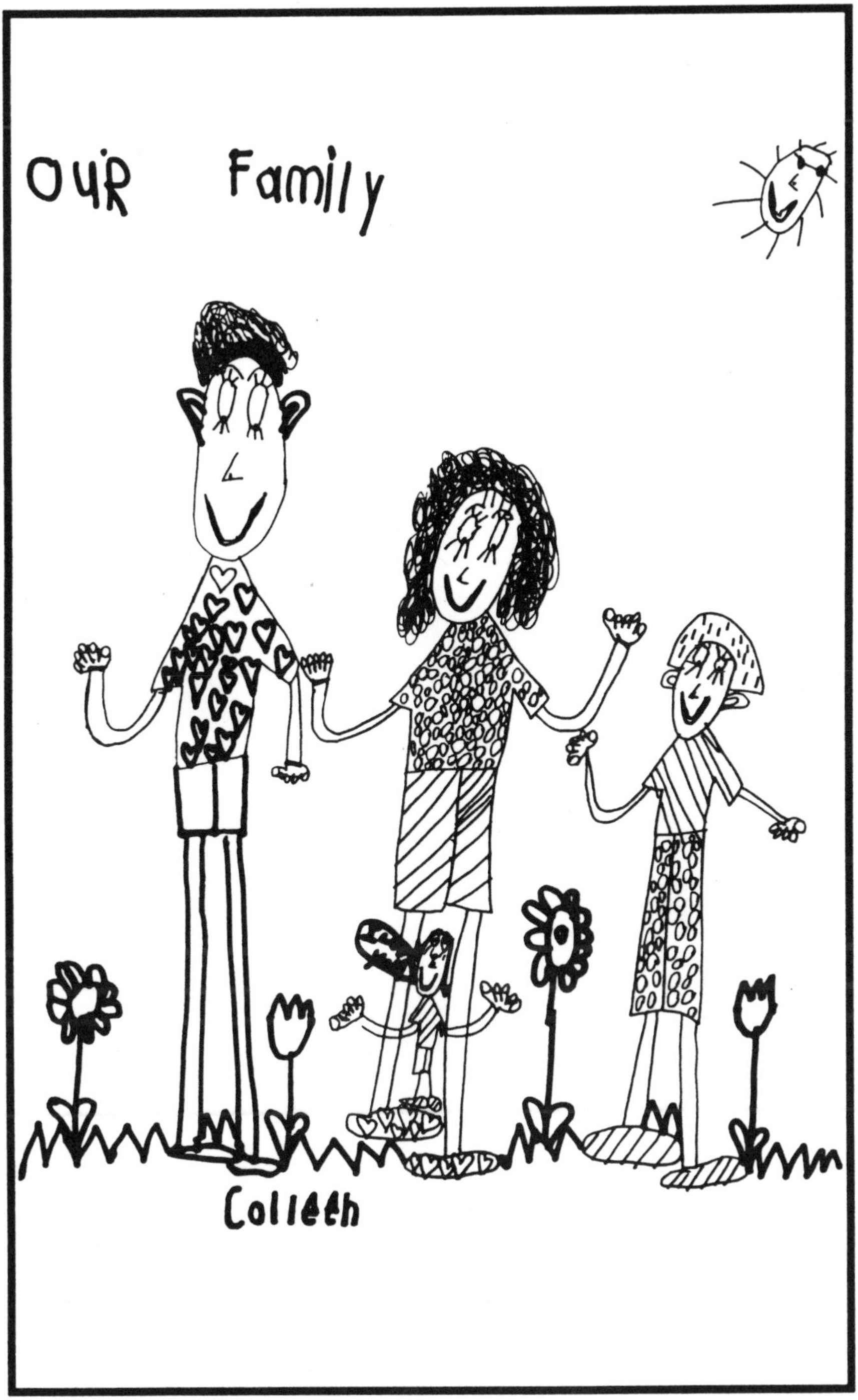
OuR Family
Colleen

INDEX

Appetizers

Soups, Stews, Salads

INDEX

Meat, Poultry, Main Dishes

Breads, Rolls, Muffins

INDEX

Desserts

Desserts

Beverages

ORDER FORM

To order additional copies of:

The Harried Housewife's Cookbook
(Easy, Quick and Delicious Recipes for the Busy Household!)

Fill in Order Form Below - Cut and Mail

Enclose check or money order for $14.95 plus $3.00 shipping and handling for one book, $1.50 for each additional book. *(New York State residents add 8% sales tax.)* Mail to:

Upstate Publishing
P.O. Box 16
Whitesboro, NY 13492-0016

Please mail_____copies of *The Harried Housewife's Cookbook* at $14.95 each, plus $3.00 shipping and handling for one book, $1.50 shipping and handling for each additional book.

Mail books to:

Name_____

Address_____

City, State, Zip_____

(Orders will be processed immediately upon receipt of payment.)